# Praise for *Quiet Leader*

'An invaluable read for introverts and e
stereotypes and illuminating the profound impact of the quiet leader.'

**Elizabeth Honer CB, former CEO of a UK
central government agency**

'Unique insights into the value introverts bring to leadership roles.
A must-read for contemporary leadership theorists.'

**Peter M. Jones, former CEO,
The Institute of Internal Auditors, Australia**

'A fantastic and easy-to-read research-based book which gives both introverts and extroverts useful tools, and helps an introvert like myself to
see that being an introvert is a strength. This book should be part of the
national curriculum! Any organisation wanting to optimise employee
performance should make this book part of their internal training.'

**Ellen Brataas, CEO, Institute of
Internal Auditors, Norway**

'I'm usually the loudest person in the room. This book made me want
to be the quietest.'

**Jill McCullough, personal impact
coach working with CEOs and multinationals**

# Quiet Leader

# Pearson

At Pearson, we have a simple mission: to help people make more of their lives through learning.

We combine innovative learning technology with trusted content and educational expertise to provide engaging and effective learning experiences that serve people wherever and whenever they are learning.

From classroom to boardroom, our curriculum materials, digital learning tools and testing programmes help to educate millions of people worldwide – more than any other private enterprise.

Every day our work helps learning flourish, and wherever learning flourishes, so do people.

To learn more, please visit us at **www.pearson.com**

# Quiet Leader

---

## What you can learn from the power of introverts

**First edition**

Sissel Heiberg

### Pearson

Harlow, England • London • New York • Boston • San Francisco • Toronto • Sydney
Dubai • Singapore • Hong Kong • Tokyo • Seoul • Taipei • New Delhi
Cape Town • São Paulo • Mexico City • Madrid • Amsterdam • Munich • Paris • Milan

**PEARSON EDUCATION LIMITED**
KAO Two
KAO Park
Harlow CM17 9NA
United Kingdom
Tel: +44 (0)1279 623623
Web: www.pearson.com

**First published 2024** (print and electronic)

© Pearson Education Limited 2024 (print and electronic)

The right of Sissel Heiberg to be identified as author of this work has been asserted by her in accordance with the Copyright, Designs and Patents Act 1988.

ISBN: 978-1-292-46215-8 (print)
       978-1-292-73032-5 (ePub)

**British Library Cataloguing-in-Publication Data**
A catalogue record for the print edition is available from the British Library

**Library of Congress Cataloging-in-Publication Data**
Names: Heiberg, Sissel, author.
Title: Quiet leader : what you can learn from the power of introverts / Sissel Heiberg.
Description: First edition. | Harlow, England ; New York : Pearson, 2024. | Includes bibliographical references and index.
Identifiers: LCCN 2024036548 | ISBN 9781292462158 (paperback) | ISBN 9781292730325 (epub)
Subjects: LCSH: Leadership--Psychological aspects. | Introverts. | Introversion.
Classification: LCC HD57.7 .H3985 2024 | DDC 658.4/092--dc23/eng/20240819
LC record available at https://lccn.loc.gov/2024036548

10 9 8 7 6 5 4 3 2 1
28 27 26 25 24

Cover designer Kelly Miller

Print edition typeset in 10/14 Charter ITC Pro by Straive
Printed in the UK by Bell and Bain Ltd, Glasgow

NOTE THAT ANY PAGE CROSS REFERENCES REFER TO THE PRINT EDITION

# Contents

———

Contents

# About the author

Sissel Heiberg is an internal audit leader with almost 20 years of experience from global financial services companies including Lloyds Banking Group, Aviva and Deutsche Bank. She holds a BA in English and International Market Communication from Norway, her native country, an MA in International Business Management from Newcastle University, and an MSc in International Relations from London School of Economics. She's a qualified accountant (ACCA), holds the project management qualification PMP and is a Certified Internal Auditor. She recently left financial services to found Foss & Bjørn, a sensory jewellery business, where she is owner and Managing Director. She lives in East London with her fiancé and their baby son.

# Acknowledgements

Before I started writing this book, I'd been told that writing is a teamwork exercise, but I don't think I'd fully grasped what that really meant – I'd pictured myself sitting in my East London loft tapping away all alone. As my partner can confirm, there was an awful lot of that too, but when I started writing I realised how much of the content was shaped by what I'd learned through interactions and experiences with others over the years; my own as well as stories kindly shared by former colleagues and other quiet leaders (all anonymised). They've all fed into the thinking that would become the ideas behind the quiet leader concept. The intelligent and thoughtful women in my non-fiction book club often steered me towards books I wouldn't otherwise have considered, and I'm grateful for the interesting conversations we have over brunch once a month. Be gentle when you discuss this one! My editor, Eloise Cook, also deserves a big thank you for providing feedback throughout and making the end product better than it was at the start – as do the rest of the Pearson team. Any errors or omissions are of course mine alone. I'd also like to thank my parents for instilling in me a love of books from an early age – I'm sure the many book subscriptions they funded, and the regular trips to the local library in Norway with my mother as a small child, are key to why this book exists at all. And thank you of course also to you, reader, for being interested enough in the topic to come on the quiet leader journey with me.

The biggest thank you, however, goes to my fiancé Steve. We found out that I was pregnant shortly after I started writing this book in earnest, and our son was 4 months old when I finished. It would've been much harder to simultaneously be a new first-time mum as well as a first-time author if you hadn't been by my side. I'm very lucky to get to spend my life with you. Thank you for everything you do for us and for everything you are.

# What brought us here

This is a book borne from frustration. After almost 20 years in increasingly senior positions in complex, large international companies, I've observed time and time again that there are some key skills we claim to value highly – and most leadership books on the market extol their virtue – but that in practice aren't the skills we actually recognise and encourage. Instead, the loudness of the extrovert is seen as a virtue, despite evidence that loudness doesn't equal quality of leadership or ability to achieve results. The fallacy that a good leader is loud is a construct perpetuated over many years, but the good news is that we can, like a wonky IKEA wardrobe, de-construct the framework the fallacy is built on and re-design it the way we want. This book is an attempt at creating a revised model for the modern high-performer, where the best results are achieved when we allow our colleagues to be who they really are, where we leverage everyone's individual strengths and where the quieter, introverted people in the room are valued for the significant contributions they make, regardless of what they look or sound like.

This book is for everyone who's been told they need to be louder in order to get ahead; it's for current and aspiring leaders who are tired of feeling like their natural approach isn't good enough; it's for those who intuitively understand that there's more than one way to be a strong leader; and it's a book for the loud leaders who realise their inherent skills aren't always the right tools for the job. This book is for everyone who believes that being quiet (but not silent) is a superpower. This book was borne out of frustration, but at its heart it is a book hoping that things can be different. Because you don't have to be loud to be a great leader.

In Part 1, I explore where the fallacy came from that a leader has to be loud, explain why in today's environment this outdated view no longer serves us and set out the argument for a different approach where we elevate leadership and value the skills of the quiet leader. For simplicity I call this the introvert/extrovert continuum, but these aren't black and white categories where you're either one or the other and where all people in one category are the same; it's a spectrum of preferred behaviours and we're all a unique combination of our genes and our environment (more on this in Chapter 1). Whether you call it introversion or something else, the label is less relevant than the idea that to enhance performance we need to hear from many different types of people who think and see the world in different ways.

It's the leader's responsibility to drive high performance by creating an environment where everyone can thrive, and consciously choose the behaviour that leads to the outcome we want. When I say leadership, I mean this in its widest sense: Regardless of what title you hold or how many people you manage, anyone can be a role model and lead an organisation in a more enlightened direction, provided you're willing to stand up for what you believe in. This might mean being different until more people catch on.

To arrive at the conclusions of this book, I've read materials in areas ranging from psychology, history, neuroscience, through to secular Buddhism, and leveraged my own experience as well as that of numerous individuals who took the time to be interviewed for this book and those who shared their experiences long before I knew there would be a book. This has given me a perspective that's a little different: Most books and training materials about introversion focus on why and how the quiet person should change, that we need to become louder in order to be more successful.[1] But when you look beyond the assumptions we've been taught to hold for so long, as we'll do in Chapter 2, there's no reason why the quiet leader needs to be loud and we certainly don't need to be 'fixed'. This isn't to say that we shouldn't all aspire to be better versions of ourselves and we all have areas where we can learn and grow – and Chapter 5 explains how we should all consciously use the behaviours that work for us in any given situation – but for most quiet leaders there's no reason to re-wire our personalities and fundamentally change our behaviour. In fact, when you look at what leading business thinkers have been saying for decades (which I cover in Chapter 3), it's clear that many of the leadership skills they're showcasing are ones that introverts find it easier to tap into. Because this ties into the wider conversation about organisational diversity, which I expand to include diversity of personality and behaviours, Chapter 4 creates a linkage between more frequent use of the quiet leader's skills and improved diversity, equity and inclusion more broadly. My argument is that having more proud quiet leaders will improve leadership for all and allow genuine diversity of thought to flourish.

This isn't a book claiming that all introverts are better leaders; like so much it comes down to the individual and their combination of skills, attributes and experiences. I do, however, want to showcase what the quiet leader adds, and how everyone's leadership abilities would improve if the quiet leader's natural skillset was leveraged more consistently by a larger group. There are too many different leadership traits for one person to excel at all of them, but the quiet leader has a natural head start in several areas key in today's ideas- and people-driven world. If our organisations start to value these, and expand our view of what good looks like, we'll increase the expectation on all leaders and elevate leadership across the board, making our organisations stronger and better able to meet the challenges ahead.

Part 2 dives into the many strengths that the quiet leader brings to the table and that everyone would benefit from leveraging more in their own toolkit. I've focused on reflection, self-awareness, empathy, calmness, humility and the ability to listen and closely observe, based on research from existing books and other written published materials, as well as interviews I've had with senior executives and input from my own online survey. Part 2 goes through each of a quiet leader's primary strengths, explains why they are key skills in today's organisations, and if you're not a natural introvert it also shows how you can develop these skills for yourself and improve your own effectiveness in a modern business environment.

If you're an extrovert[2] reading this, I hope this book encourages you to leverage your quiet skills more to elevate your leadership practice – your quiet colleagues can perhaps access them more easily, but you also have them. It requires some work, but I've included exercises and self-reflection steps in each chapter to make the journey a bit easier. If you're an introvert, my goal is that I save you time and frustration, showcase what you add and highlight that it's the system that needs to change, not you – that you'll get to the end of this book and appreciate what you add more than you did before you started reading.

It's my hope that the quiet leaders who come after me, and my peers who are currently out there feeling different, will realise that there's nothing wrong with being yourself at work. Knowing who you are and having the confidence to be yourself is invaluable, and if enough of us become more in tune with our quiet side, the system will change for the better, one interaction and one quiet leader at a time.

# part 1

—

# Introversion at work

# chapter 1

---

# Are you an introvert?

If you were told that someone is an introvert, what images would
that conjure up in your mind? Perhaps someone who doesn't say
much, maybe someone who keeps themselves to themselves, a bit
outside the main crowd? If that's what you picture, you're not alone.
Introversion is a much-misunderstood and misused term; it's often
conflated with being 'shy'. Some consider it to be about the source
of someone's energy; some believe it's about how much time we
can spend with others before we need 'alone time'; yet others don't
believe in the concept of introversion at all, often using themselves
as an example because they're very outgoing in some situations and
more reserved in others.

There are many different ways to interpret what introversion is,
so to have a sensible conversation about what someone on the introverted spectrum brings to a leadership role and what others can
learn from their behavioural preferences, I'll first define what
I mean when I say 'introversion' in this book. That will help me
make sure I get my message across, and it'll help you when you read
this book as you'll have a better sense of where I'm coming from. If
I talk about a quiet leader and I picture someone in a small crowd
speaking confidently about a topic they know inside-out, and you

picture a wallflower hiding in a corner, the next few chapters will get confusing very quickly because of our different starting points. This first chapter therefore delves into introversion as a concept, sets out what I mean with the word 'introversion' and explains what the available research tells us (and what we don't yet know), including some myth busting, since it's only when we have a collective understanding of terminology that we can really start to have meaningful dialogue (spoken like a true introvert).

## What does introversion mean?

Introversion, as a word as well as a concept, is hard to agree on partly due to the lack of research. Additionally, in the conversations I had with quiet leaders as part of the preparation for this book, their emphasis often differed in which aspect of introversion resonated with them personally. But before we delve into the various views of what introversion is, let's go back to basics and look at the word itself: Intro-version. It first appeared in 1654, as an offshoot of 'introspection'. The word is made up of two parts: 'intro' from the Latin word 'introvere' meaning 'within' and 'version' from the Latin 'vertere' meaning 'to turn'.[1] Etymologically speaking, an introvert is therefore someone focused on their own internal world, as opposed to an extrovert who's more externally centred. When Googling introversion, the definition that comes up is 'the quality of being shy and reticent', with an example of someone saying 'I'm an introvert and I don't like public speaking'. The *Merriam-Webster Dictionary* lists 'wallflower' as a synonym, and *Oxford English Dictionary* considers an introvert someone who's 'withdrawn or reserved'.

In these definitions there's clearly a tendency to conflate introversion with being vocal and taking action, as indicated in the words 'shy' and 'speaking'. However, in the words of Malcolm Gladwell, **speaking is not an act of extroversion.**[2] Whether someone is willing or able to speak publicly doesn't say anything about their personality, how they feel about public speaking, nor about how they assess their own performance during or afterwards.

There are numerous examples of self-categorised introverts in the public eye who, if willingness to speak publicly was a limitation, wouldn't be in the position they're in, including Gwyneth Paltrow, Harrison Ford, Keanu Reeves and Steve Martin, to name a few, as well as experts in their fields used to using their voices to persuade others and gain influence, such as investor Warren Buffet, former prime minister Winston Churchill and former *Washington Post* owner Katharine Graham (portrayed by Meryl Streep, herself an introvert, in the 2017 film *The Post*).[3] Being an introvert therefore doesn't have any bearing on whether someone is in the public eye or on whether they work in professions that require large amounts of people interaction.

The misunderstanding that introversion equals shyness limits our understanding of each other. Being shy or not enjoying public speaking relates to emotions – how a situation makes a person *feel*. Introversion, however, is a matter of temperament, of personality and behavioural preference. It's perfectly possible to be extroverted and shy – some research has indicated that extroverts are in fact *more* likely to feel shy as it arises when you're wanting to connect, but find it difficult; an introvert who prefers to spend more time alone might not always want the connection in the first place.[4] It might well be the case that someone is an introvert and their behavioural preference is to avoid public speaking because it causes them a feeling of anxiety; however, someone else who's also introverted might thrive in the public eye. The two lenses are different and are unrelated to each other – a bit like someone who's introverted and loves dark chocolate, or an introvert who prefers milk chocolate (like myself); the personality trait of introversion is not a relevant factor in their preference for milk chocolate over dark. Similarly, an introvert can also be very comfortable with public speaking.[5]

## Nature or nurture

In recent years, more research (though still not enough) has been undertaken into the origin of personalities, and as a result we now have improved language to understand better what distinguishes temperament and personality, and mood from emotion, which helps the conversation.[6] This is important because introversion so often gets confused with feelings and behaviours that are negative in a work context, such as shyness and anxiety. The differences between these categories can be broadly summarised as outlined below.

- **Mood:** A state of mind that can last for minutes or hours, and may or may not be affected by a person's environment (such as playing a happy song to lift your spirits, or lighting a candle for romance).

- **Emotion:** A feeling lasting seconds or minutes (shorter in duration than moods), connected to a particular situation or experience. Like mood, emotions can also be triggered by the environment, for instance a song that brings back a particular memory. Shyness or nervousness are both emotions that lead to a particular behaviour (such as avoiding public speaking). Emotions can affect mood, and vice versa.

- **Behavioural preference:** A default behaviour, from being used frequently because the behaviour provides a particular benefit to the user or because it's a born trait. Preferences aren't static and can change – and be changed – over time.

- **Temperament:** Something you're born with, and stays with you irrespective of experiences throughout your life.

- **Personality trait:** What you're shaped by over the course of a lifetime, including experiences and interactions you have.

We're all a unique mixture of our upbringing and the environment we're in. In this sense, the idea of introversion spans both nature (temperament) and nurture (personality), and leads to behavioural preferences. Many books have been written about the impact of nature and nurture, and how they interrelate, though for our purposes I'll focus on the end result, which is that an introvert – regardless of the reason for the introversion – has a preference for certain types of behaviour over others. Extroverts similarly have their own set of default behaviours.

# What does the science tell us?

Many have opinions about introversion and extroversion based on speculation and anecdotes rather than scientific study and experiments, and it'll take time before the many misconceptions are cleared up, simply because more research is needed. Jung's theories that form the basis for the Myers Briggs personality tests, for instance, are widely used but also controversial.[7] It doesn't help that introversion is generally only seen in relation to extroversion, as its opposite, and not defined on its own terms (the famous Big 5 personality traits assess individuals for 'degrees of extroversion', not introversion specifically). This limits our understanding of leadership, just like the assumption that male is the default limits our understanding of gender.[8] Introversion needs to be defined in its own way and not just as the opposite of extroversion; we lose something in translation when we see the world through an extroverted default lens, and we assume that other behavioural preferences are deviations rather than valid – and sometimes better – options. This again leads to organisational losses through missed opportunities for improved performance at the individual and the collective level. (Given I just used gender as an example of where there's a default similar to the extrovert default, you might be thinking that introversion is more common in women, but let me just dispel that straight-away: There's no evidence that there are more female introverts, and a study from 1996 of both men and women actually shows that introversion is slightly more common than extroversion across both genders.[9])

Professor Jonathan Cheek and his team have attempted to make more scientific some of the language around introversion. They've identified four types of introverts (Social, Thinking, Anxious and Restrained – handily coming together as the acronym STAR). Often, one individual belongs in more than one category at the same time, and this multidimensional view helps us to be mindful that not every introvert is the same – introverts are individuals, just like extroverts, though the former may be placed under more scrutiny and analysis.

Although based on a limited population, the four types are a good starting point for making a 'woolly' topic more research based, and can help us narrow down exactly what we mean when we talk about introversion.[10] Common for all of introverts is that there's a need for time *between* interactions or activities, whereas extroverts need time *inside* the interaction for refuelling.[11]

- **Social introvert:** Someone whose introversion first and foremost comes across in their preference to limit social interaction – they need space to themselves after interactions and prefer to meet 1-2-1 or in smaller groups. Traditionally, extroverts have been seen as highly sociable and – since introverts tend to be defined not in relation to what an introvert is, but as the opposite of a sociable extrovert – there's a tendency to think that introverts are anti-people. This is of course not the case; a social introvert still likes people, has a human need for connection, and still takes pleasure from interacting with others – it's simply that the method, volume and ways in which that interaction takes place differ from the extrovert. It's also important to note that for the social introvert this is a behavioural preference and not a result of social anxiety. Helgoe gives the example that extroverts are like chain hotels with lots of rooms for lots of people; they have lots of social interactions but may not give full attention to any particular one. In contrast, the social introvert is more like a classy boutique hotel where each interaction has its luxurious and spacious suite; there are fewer rooms (fewer social interactions), but each one is given complete focus, and the total available (brain) space is the same.[12]

- **Thinking introvert:** This is someone who doesn't have the behavioural preference to limit social interaction in the way of the social introvert; they happily engage in large groups, and don't need to withdraw in order to recover after social interactions. They need adequate time to reflect and think, and do activities that enable them to fill their introvert needs such as meditating, painting or journalling (or writing a book). This means they still prefer more time alone than an extrovert; however, the reason for this preference is to enable a focus on their thoughts and inner life rather than to recharge from the volume or length of social interactions. For both the social and the thinking introvert, their time alone supports their energy-refuelling need.

- **Anxious introvert:** Creek and team defined this type as someone who wants solitude and avoids social interactions because of the way it makes them feel. They're likely to be insecure and lacking in confidence, and will ruminate on an interaction long after it's passed. This is a controversial type since, as you know from earlier, the behavioural preference of introversion and the feeling of anxiety are two different things. Further research is needed to understand whether a higher proportion of introverts also suffer from anxiety; however, we do know that being an extrovert is no guarantee for a life free from anxiety, social or otherwise.

- **Restrained introvert:** These are introverts who prefer to take things slowly and who like to keep their activities to a minimum. They aren't necessarily interested in seeking out new and exciting experiences, preferring instead to stick to the tried and tested. They operate at a slightly slower pace than others and are most comfortable when there isn't too much going on around them. Again, more research is needed to understand how large a proportion of individuals this covers.

The research team found that, as in so many other parts of life, introverts are often a mixture of categories and no single person is one-dimensional. The groups above are still work in progress and arguably confuse behavioural preferences with feelings; however, they're an important step in introducing more scientific rigour to the conversation. This also helps us when discussing introversion in leadership because we can start to think about the people around us in a more nuanced way that allows us to see the benefits of introversion and makes it easier to identify the introverted behaviours that add value: the colleague who observed that a stakeholder didn't seem as enthusiastic as expected, leading to an after-meeting follow-up and avoiding the loss of a major client, or the colleague who thought through the consequences of holding a press conference about a new product on the same day that our company received a regulatory fine. Previously our attention might have been on the introvert who is slow to respond and never says anything in meetings. Now, however, we have language enabling us to focus on the positive contributions of the introvert and this enables us to recognise what quiet leaders can add. I'm not saying that all types of introverts are better leaders than extroverts, but that introverts bring key skills to the table that shouldn't be dismissed and are key for the success of today's organisations.

In addition to clearer language for discussing introversion, we now also have improved technology to better understand how the human brain works. More and more research is being done to help explore how neurological differences impact our behavioural preferences.[13] Though this is still a relatively new area, several studies have shown that people who self-identify as introverts have higher levels of blood flowing to, and higher levels of electrical activity in, the areas of the brain that deal with memory, planning and problem solving. Extroverts, on the other hand, have elevated blood flow volume to areas responsible for visual, auditory and sensory processing.[14] The areas where the blood flows are the more active areas so this helps explain why introverts are naturally more focused on internal experiences and extroverts have a more outward focus; this is where our brains spend effort. One study even showed higher levels of activity overall in the brains of introverts, helping to explain why introverts have an increased need to recharge and shut out external inputs, as they're distractions taking away focus from the high levels of activity inside.[15] So, rather than being low action, the introvert brain is actually already full of activity, completely the opposite of how many perceive us! Quiet people have the loudest minds, indeed.

The work relating to blood flow has been enhanced with research on the human nervous system – which regulates temperature, emotion, health, thirst and a whole host of other important functions – and these show that the *para*sympathetic nervous system (which helps calm us down) is more dominant in introverts. Extroverts have a more dominant sympathetic nervous system, which is the brain's 'higher gear' causing them to seek action, activity and new experiences. This desire for adrenaline also comes from the extrovert's high need for dopamine. Dopamine – the brain's 'reward centre' and the little voice that tells us to keep doing something because it feels good – is found in introverts and extroverts alike, and we all need it in a Goldilocks-style balancing act of 'not too much and not too little'. Extroverts, however, are very sensitive to the positive emotions that follow when they get a dopamine hit (which lights up a part of the brain called the ventral tegmental area and specifically the nucleus accumbens), which causes them to continue to seek out situations that provide it, in addition to dopamine being key to the neurotransmitter pathway that extroverts rely on. The neurotransmitter pathway that introverts default to also gives positive psychological reward, but it has a lower dependency on adrenalin-fuelled dopamine, so introverts get less benefit back from seeking out the activities that extroverts thrive on. Seeking out more dopamine would overload the introvert's nervous system, whereas the extrovert goes 'more, more, more' to get the same good feeling that reading a good book gives an introvert.[16]

That's a lot of science, so to help keep track of it all, I've included Table 1.1 to summarise the differences between introverts and extroverts as identified from brain imaging using electroencephalography (EEG – brain waves), positron emission tomography (PET) and functional magnetic resonance imaging (fMRI) to see which brain areas are activated when performing different tasks. This is a relatively new field and more research is needed; however, Table 1.1 outlines what we know so far.

**Table 1.1** Summary of differences between introverts and extroverts as identified through brain scanning

| Brain imaging results | Introvert | Extrovert |
|---|---|---|
| More active parts of brain (measured as blood flowing to) | Parts responsible for internal experiences like planning, solving problems, memory – internal to us | Parts responsible for visuals, auditory stimulation and touch – external to us |
| Dominant neurotransmitter and pathway | Acetylcholine, with a longer and more complex pathway (goes via Broca's area for inner monologue, frontal lobe for reasoning and learning, hippocampus for long-term memory, and anterior thalamus which again sends stimuli to the frontal lobe) | Dopamine pathway, shorter and more direct (doesn't go via Broca's area and frontal lobe, but rather via temporal and motor area responsible for actions, and via posterior thalamus, which sends stimuli to amygdala which connects actions with emotions – the 'thinking fast'/system 1 that I talk about in chapter 2) |
| Blood flow volume overall | Higher, especially in the frontal cortex | Lower |
| Dominant nervous system | Parasympathetic, responsible for calming us down | Sympathetic, responsible for increasing adrenaline |
| Dopamine and positive emotional responsiveness | Lower psychological reward for seeking out high-adrenaline situations, and lower reactions in the ventral tegmental area and nucleus accumbens when positive reward is imminent | High dopamine need, meaning they need more to activate their neurotransmitter pathway, and high emotional responsiveness to positive external stimuli.[17] Also high response in the ventral tegmental area and the nucleus accumbens when positive reward is imminent |

# Are you an introvert?

Using these inputs, I've fine-tuned the definition of introversion I use in this book so we're all on the same page cover to cover: Introversion is the extent to which a person experiences and interacts with the world along the dimensions outlined below.

- How much you're energised and get a 'dopamine hit' through solitude or the company of others (i.e. how you respond to external stimuli): An introvert is more likely to want downtime on their own or in small groups, whereas an extrovert prefers to be with a larger group and recharges their energy that way. To reiterate, an introvert needs time *between* interactions, and an extrovert needs time *inside* the interaction.

- Whether you prefer to observe and reflect deeply before speaking and doing: An introvert is more likely to think through their words and ideas end to end before speaking, and enjoy the process of doing so, whereas an extrovert uses the act of talking as part of their thinking process.

You'll notice that the above says 'the extent to which' for both dimensions. This is intentional, to recognise that introversion and extroversion exist on a spectrum and nobody is always entirely one or the other. It's a rare individual who's at either extreme end of the scale at any time. You might slide to one or the other side depending on the particular circumstances of a particular day, and you as an individual will have a range that you can't go beyond and this range is different from those around you. For simplicity, I'll still use 'introvert' and 'extrovert' (it's far easier than 'behavioural preferences of those of us defaulting to introversion'), but this doesn't mean we're always talking about the far end of the scale. It's always a continuum and not completely fixed.[18]

You're more likely to be an introvert ('have behavioural preferences defaulting to introversion') if you answer Yes to the following questions.

- Do you prefer conversation and interaction 1-2-1 and in smaller groups?
- Are you comfortable spending time on your own?
- Do you need time away from others after being in larger groups?
- Do you find it easy to see things from other people's perspectives, even if you don't necessarily agree with them?
- Have you been told you're a good listener?
- Do you tend to notice things that other people don't?
- Do you feel like you're being 'put on the spot' if you have to give an opinion without the opportunity to think it through? (Note that even the most introverted of souls might not feel this way if they're asked for an opinion on a topic they feel is straightforward and doesn't need much nuanced assessment.)
- Do you rarely act impulsively?
- Have you found that others make assumptions about you that may be incorrect because you don't always share a lot of personal information about yourself?
- Do you enjoy spending time reflecting and analysing?

As you can tell, there are many different giveaways to indicate whether you're an introvert or not, what type you are, and where on the spectrum you might find yourself. Given the nuances involved and since no two people are alike, and since introversion isn't a category that most people can easily be placed into simply from observation, some people don't believe that introversion exists at all. Often during my conversations with those who doubt its existence, it transpires that they're more easily able to move across the spectrum with a wide behavioural range, or that they haven't considered how the activity of a particular day affects them. They might say 'but I'm sometimes loud and sometimes quiet' and argue that this means introversion doesn't exist – when of course introverts can be gregarious and entertaining in the right context. It's important that we don't pigeonhole each other; however, an individual's experience of where they see themselves on the introversion/extroversion continuum on a particular day depending on circumstances doesn't preclude us from identifying certain patterns of behaviour that arise from the introvert traits we defined above.[19]

## Internalising the perception of others

I don't know how many times people have expressed surprise when I declare myself to be an introvert – usually the response is something like 'I'd never have guessed it – you're so outgoing!' The misunderstandings that introversion can easily be seen from the outside and that we don't like to spend time with people perpetuate the impression that an introvert can't be a good leader, since leading is such a people-oriented business. It's easy to be flattered when you're singled out like this, to be seen as different than 'the other introverts', but it does us a disservice in the long run. When a boy tells a girl 'you're not like the other girls' to make her feel special and valued, there's an implicit judgement about the others; that they're not worth his time because they're girls and the one he's singled out is, *despite* being one. Similarly, if we feel flattered to be labelled different from other introverts, we're perpetuating the idea that being an introvert is a negative and that introverts are 'less than'. This means we silently agree that introverts aren't capable of being good leaders. I've fallen for this myself many times, and several of the introvert leaders I talked to during the research for this book did the same – when I asked them how they see introversion manifesting itself in their own behaviours, the vast majority caveated their responses by saying 'I'm not a typical introvert'. This shows how we've all internalised some of the negative messages about introversion in business. The sooner we educate ourselves about what introversion really is and what it looks like (and how it differs from shyness and other negatively loaded words), the sooner we understand what introversion in leadership adds. This will also help us and those around us see the benefits of choosing introverted behaviours in a business and leadership context regardless of whether you self-identify as an introvert or not.[20]

The misunderstandings around introversion do us a major disservice: it affects how we're perceived as leaders or of leadership potential. If being an introvert is the same as being shy or have a dislike for public speaking, how can you be effective in business? How can you persuade, sell and present your case convincingly if you're too anxious or timid to voice your opinion? How can you inspire others if you're unable to state to the world what your beliefs are? You can see how it's easy to think that an introvert is unable to be an effective leader if you believe in these common misconceptions.

This is not to say that all introverts are good leaders, nor that all extroverts are poor ones – they do, however, bring different things to the table that organisations would benefit from valuing equally and in a balanced way. Each comes with behavioural preferences that have consequences for the organisation and for those in a leader's charge. In a few chapters' time we'll start to explore the behaviours that come more easily to someone on the introverted spectrum, and how they improve the performance of the organisation, especially if they're recognised and consciously adopted not just by introverts but by everyone.

## A warning about categories

Having defined introversion for ourselves, we should also be mindful that categorisation, by its very definition – although useful as a shortcut – provides a less refined view of the world than what we see in real life. Categorisation of individuals will therefore always be flawed and we shouldn't assume that each person in a category is the same or that each individual behaves in the same way consistently. There are, however, some behaviours that are more likely to be represented in those on the introverted end of the scale than others, such as a need for quietness. This doesn't mean that all introverts are quiet all the time, and there might even be variation within a single day depending on what else is going on in that person's world. Categories and definitions help us, but we need to also understand where they hold us back or mislead. This awareness, the language we use to interpret and understand those around us, the context in which we see each other and what we associate with the categories we use, all matter a great deal. We'll explore this in Chapter 2 as I move on to the bias inherent in some of the language around introversion and the impact this has on workplace dynamics.

# A section for self-reflection

- - - - - - - - - - - - - - - - - - - - - - - - - - - - - - - - - - - - - -

- Which communication method do you prefer when you want to interact with someone? Where do you think that preference comes from?

- How often do you reflect on what you're looking for from an interaction before it starts?

- Have you asked those around you how they see you? How did their responses relate to your own view of yourself? If you've not asked anyone this question, why not?

- Who are the people in your professional life you get on best with? What is it that makes those relationships work well?

- - - - - - - - - - - - - - - - - - - - - - - - - - - - - - - - - - - - - -

# chapter 2

---

# Why we're biased in favour of extroverts

We now have a joint understanding of what we mean by 'introversion', so let's move on to look at how the behaviours associated with introversion are seen in organisations today. I mentioned in Chapter 1 that the words we use affect how individuals are perceived. This has implications for how people with introvert traits are treated in the workplace and reflects a bias that affects which behaviours are considered desirable. This chapter explores what this means in practice, what the extrovert bias is and why the negative perception of introverts appeared in the first place. We often talk about bias in the context of visible traits, such as race, gender and disability; however, it's much broader than that.

## Absence is hard to see

It's harder to see something hidden than to see what's right in front of you, and the process of *doing* (commonly associated with extroversion) is very observable. The process of *reflection* (usually associated with introversion) is less obvious.[1] This, added to the fact that some of the behavioural traits of introversion – being thoughtful, calm and quiet – are also 'hidden', increases the perception that introversion means absence. In this way, an introvert becomes the person whose words are absent and actions missing. In a society biased towards talking, with visible action-based skills more highly valued, where it matters less whether the words spoken are meaningful and whether the actions taken are the right ones, a person who reflects before making a decision is seen as devoid of action and will be compared negatively with the person who makes an immediate decision. It matters less whether the decision is the right one.[2] We value what we can easily see and hear. The lack of external cues, however, doesn't mean that there's nothing going on, as shown in Figure 2.1. (I'll show in more detail later that these are active behaviours in their own right.)

As we saw in Chapter 1, introversion is generally defined as the opposite of extroversion. This means that introversion is the absence of extroverted traits, rather than being defined in its own right. Even professionals who should know better do this – you might have heard of the 'Big 5' personality traits, which is used in all manner of personality assessments, including recruitment into some of the world's largest companies.[3] The 'Big 5' considers personality along five different dimensions, one of which is 'extent of extroversion'.[4] There's no 'extent of introversion' equivalent – introversion is simply the absence of extroversion; extroversion is defined by what it is, introversion is defined by what it isn't (extroversion). We also see this in the *Oxford English Dictionary*, where an introvert is defined as 'the opposite of an extrovert'. There's no such reference to extroversion being the opposite of introversion, even though they're two sides of the same coin.[5]

As a result of this perception that introversion is the absence of something made present by extroversion, and the difficulty we have as humans in seeing something that we think isn't there, extroversion becomes the default simply because it's easier for us to observe (there's also an element of primal behaviour going on, as I'll show later in this chapter). So what impact does it have on our perception of introversion that extroversion is seen as the default?

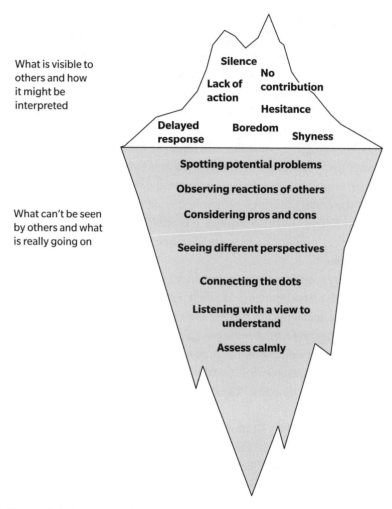

**Figure 2.1** Introverts have lots going on that isn't immediately visible with the naked eye

## Simple minds

According to nudge theory, the default automatically becomes the preferred choice and is usually considered the 'better' option.[6] A famous example is the English government's approach to increasing the number of organ donors: By changing the default option to 'opt out' and presuming consent to becoming a donor, instead of the previous 'opt in', the number of donors increased drastically. Because humans are inherently working from the default position, the outcome can be manipulated depending on what the starting point is. In the organ donation scenario, the government wanted more donations and thus set the default to be 'opt in'. Those who feel strongly against this still have the option to say no and change away from the default. Few do, however, because of the human tendency towards inertia and to see the default as 'normal'. What the default is therefore matters: what's seen as normal is more desirable, and also requires less energy since making active decisions is hard work and we tend to want to make our lives as easy as possible.

Another example of the importance of the default is the use of male crash test dummies in seatbelt tests; when more women were hurt in car accidents it was seen as evidence that women were more fragile, when in fact car seats weren't designed or tested on women, whose anatomy is different to men's. That's what led to a higher number of serious injuries in women over men, not an inherent fragility in the female body.[7] The default can have major implications in many ways.

The story of Hilary Clinton is a good example of the implications of the default in a leadership context. To summarise, she was a US senator from 2001 to 2009, Secretary of State from 2009 to 2013, and ran for the Presidency in the 2016 election, making her the first female to win a presidential nomination for one of the two major US parties.[8] The feedback she received when she lost was that she wasn't 'presidential enough'. [9] With no precedent, as there had never before been a female US President, of course this is in one sense accurate – she didn't look or act like prior presidents.[10] She would have, if she'd been elected, been unlike any other president, as they have all so far in history been male. In this sense Clinton was clearly not presidential, since it would be defined in this narrow sense as 'male'. Our minds, unfortunately, are not able to easily distinguish between 'not presidential' as a result of her being the first of her kind, and 'not presidential' due to skills and capability.[11] We can't of course say whether she'd have been a good president, but the point is there was an assumption made about her abilities because she was unlike the 'standard'.

The phenomenon that these examples highlight also occurs in the introvert/extrovert relationship: Because extroversion is seen as the default, we assume that extroversion is the better approach and that extroverted behaviours give the best results and should be emulated – which affects decisions made about individuals such as performance appraisals and promotions. We look for, and find, evidence that extroverts are better leaders, without looking at the underlying assumptions forming the basis for our thinking.

## What's in a name?

The words we use reinforce this impression that extroversion is 'better'. An extrovert might be described as gregarious, but could also be referred to as too loud; they might talk more than listen, but we rarely flag this is a problem; they might be good at small talk, but you could also say small talk is superficial and prevents people from getting to know one another at a deeper level, yet we don't call extroverts shallow. We rarely hear extroverts being described in a negative way even though extrovert traits aren't all positive; we focus overly on the positive aspects of extroversion and on the negatives with introversion.[12] A positive description of an introvert could be they're thoughtful and reflective, but we rarely hear this, just like you rarely hear someone describe an extrovert as 'too loud'. The words we use matter in defining our perception of the thing or person we describe, and it affects how we see them. Instead of describing reality, however, the language we use only accurately describes the assumptions we hold.[13] Just as we're becoming more aware of how language affects our perception around gender and race (e.g. we're more likely to use the words 'aggressive' – a negative – of a black woman instead of the more positive 'assertive'[14]), so too must we become aware of the importance of the language we use about introverts and extroverts in business. We must move away from the negative descriptions of introverts and sole focus on the positive for extroverts, because the true contribution of each type to an organisation isn't reflected in this kind of polarised language.

The words we use don't just affect how others see an individual, it also affects how they see themselves. Every single leader I interviewed for this book felt the need to caveat their introversion, even though they self-identified as one; they saw it as something they either wanted to distance themselves from, or they saw themselves as an exception to the rule, that they weren't like most other introverts. The way we talk about introversion, usually in negative terms, is so ingrained it's also been internalised by us as introverts. While understandable, this perpetuates the problem and ignores the positives of introversion's behavioural traits and the value that they can bring to an organisation. As a result, our companies are missing out, and performance isn't as high as it otherwise could have been. This internalising starts early. Introverts are from an early age told that there's something wrong with their behavioural preferences. In nurseries, children are asked questions like 'did you enjoy working in a group?' where the expected answer is clearly yes, or 'what friends have you made today?' where the expectation is that friends will have been made. Children are keen observers and notice that their louder peers get more attention and that teachers interact more often with students who dominate the conversation more readily. They carry this with them into adulthood with a feeling that quietness and introspection are something to be overcome rather than strengths to be praised and encouraged.[15]

# Our primal side

So how did extroversion become the default in the first place, other than being more immediately visible? To explore this, let's start from the beginning – and I mean the very beginning: We're all human beings. Evolutionarily speaking, we all take mental shortcuts (called 'heuristics') to make our lives easier when faced with complex situations, are under time pressure, where we're overwhelmed with too much information, or where information is missing. All of these scenarios are, of course, very common today. Back in our cave days, using heuristics helped us survive, helped us understand the world around us, and was therefore hugely valuable to us as a species. Imagine you're being hunted by a lion – your instincts would tell you that you're not able to fight this animal, so you instinctively decide to run instead. This is a decision you make, but it's not a conscious one, and it happens in a split second; your legs start to move before you're aware of the thought that you need to get away. In this scenario, you're creating a mental connection between the lion's teeth and claws, and perhaps it also makes a threatening sound. As a result, your body and mind respond according to what the shortcut is telling you to do. In this case, with a lion in front of you, it's likely that your mental shortcut is highly accurate and that you're better off running than staying put to debate with the lion the merits of vegetarianism.[16]

The part of the brain that tells us what to do in this situation, the intuitive part that doesn't require us to do any conscious thinking before recommending action, is called the amygdala. It's small, almond-shaped and sits right at the core of our brains because it was one of the first areas to develop – which explains why it focuses on core behaviours such as 'fight, flight or freeze' when we feel under threat (real or perceived, lions or colleagues). Given how evolution works, the amygdala didn't change over time from driving our instinctive behaviours to something we're in control of; our brains simply evolved to develop other, more sophisticated layers *above and around* the amygdala. This enables us to override the amygdala's 'gut feel', which causes us to make instinctive decisions, but the amygdala's immediate responses are still there and not always conscious. This is important: evolution hasn't removed the initial instincts; the amygdala and the responses it's driving are still there. We therefore need to check that we know which part of the brain we're following and not assume we're in conscious control when it's actually the amygdala ruling our perception and behaviour. You can aim to bring these unconscious aspects to the surface to ensure you make a conscious decision about the situation you're in or the person you're dealing with, but to think that you can remove the impact of the amygdala altogether doesn't align with what we know about human physiology and psychology, and will likely lead to more biased decision-making, not less. Although we've moved away from having regular interactions with lions, we haven't evolved from heuristics.

Not only is the amygdala still sitting right at the core of our brains and still a key part of our decision-making, our world remains too complex for us to be able to weigh up all pros and cons or all possible options every time we need to make a decision. There are too many demands on our time and too many distractions for this. So we all still rely on heuristics to help us make decisions – including decisions about those around us.

To do this, in the absence of better information, we use external cues that we think will help – as an example, research shows that people who are tall are perceived as better leaders than shorter individuals.[17] Perhaps in our ancient history we felt that someone taller could protect us better, and we've carried that with us so that even today we believe a tall person is a better leader than someone shorter. Other physical characteristics have also been shown to influence our perception of whether someone is a good leader or not, such as good looks.[18] These assumptions don't just have an evolutionary component; our preferences can also be taught. In *Sway: Unravelling Unconscious Bias* Agarwal describes an experiment where schoolchildren were divided into two groups based on the colour of their eyes and were told that brown-eyed children were superior to the blue-eyed ones, and allocated privileges based on eye colour (such as longer lunch breaks). It only took the children a few days before this was the default position. Brown-eyed children grew in confidence based on their privileges and started to look down on their blue-eyed peers. This type of experiment has been replicated a number of times;[19] biases can be taught, humans are malleable and our perceptions vary depending on the environment we're in.

Whether the origin of a particular bias is evolutionary or learned, mental shortcuts are critical for us to function efficiently day to day.

However, as humans we're easily fooled, and we therefore need to be aware of the types of mental shortcuts we use to reduce their impact.[20]

# A selection of biases

I once had a manager who claimed he was 'in control of his bias'. Given what we know about the amygdala, that its workings are outside conscious thought, being in control of your bias isn't possible – we can't be in control of something we're not aware of. Where possible, it's therefore important that we bring to the surface our blind spots, and take action to change them where they have negative consequences (it's unrealistic to think we can bring them all to the surface at all times, but it has to start with awareness). This is often referred to as system 1 and 2, where the former is the faster route we often call 'gut feel'. We use instinct and mental shortcuts to make quick decisions using the amygdala. System 2 is a separate, slower process where we force unconscious assumptions into the open as much as possible and consider in a more reflective way the decisions in front of us. Although there's room for both, the slower route usually leads to better decisions and higher-quality outcomes.

Most of the time biases have negative consequences.[21] Therefore, unless we make ourselves aware of them they continue to be perpetuated, and we'll continue to (wrongly) assume that being quiet means that someone is poor leadership material and that being an introvert is a negative behavioural trait, as 65 per cent did in a study by Grant, Gino and Hofmann.[22] Unless we make a conscious effort to assess our biases, we'll continue to (wrongly) assume that it takes an extrovert to be a good leader and inspire people. Self-reflection and self-awareness are key to this as they can help us counter the effects of bias. Although my manager misunderstood the concept completely, he's not alone in thinking that he's aware of his blind spots. Many of us think we're aware of the biases we hold, and sometimes we do indeed work actively to counteract them. However, there's such a wide range of ways in which our brains play tricks on us that it's hard to eliminate this effect entirely. A good starting point, however, is to educate ourselves on the biases that are likely to most affect us.

Many books have been written about heuristics more generally, and in leadership theory specifically, as mental shortcuts inevitably lead to bias in the workplace. However, for the purposes of this book, I'll focus on the shortcuts that affect our perception of quiet people. As we go through each of these biases, consider how many of these you're using to make your life easier and how many judgement errors they might have led to in your interactions with people who are quieter than you. If you're an introvert, consider whether you're self-limiting as a result of internalising the misperception that you're not a good leader because you're quiet and reflective.

• **Action bias:** We assume that action, any action, is better than no action. It doesn't matter whether the actions taken are the right ones, the human brain will see action, and the proposal to take action, as better than no action. Taking action makes us feel we're *doing* something, and this makes us feel we're not letting events overtake us, that we're changing the course of events, and that we're being proactive, which is generally seen as a good thing.[23] Say, for instance, that Tom is in a meeting about a project at risk of not meeting an imminent deadline. Tom proposes that the project manager diverts resource from another area to the group with the deadline. Martin listens to the proposal, then highlights that diverting resource will mean that the second group will be at risk of delay next month. Tom's proposal is nevertheless chosen because this solves the most immediate problem, and they resolve to tackle the resource issue at a later stage. Although it solved the first problem, Tom's knee-jerk reaction created more new problems which could have been avoided if they'd deliberated more before a decision was made. (I intentionally use the negative language 'knee-jerk' here to describe Tom's approach – in reality, given the language biases we discussed earlier, Tom's approach is more likely to be referred to as 'decisive'.)
  Action bias is perpetuated because people who propose action are generally not penalised if those actions don't pan out in

the way the proposer intended. This is because a group rarely reflects on whether the actions were the right ones and, in meetings, errors are rarely highlighted and contradicted openly. An extrovert might make a factually inaccurate statement, but we generally prefer to avoid highlighting these errors to avoid embarrassing a colleague in front of others. To counteract this bias, it's therefore important that decision-making slows down and that all voices in the room are listened to.

- **Primacy effect:** First impressions count and human beings easily let ourselves be led by the first person voicing an opinion in a group setting. This bias is why introverted leaders are often advised by executive coaches to make a statement early on in a meeting. The intent behind this is good; it's so that the introverted leader becomes part of the conversation and doesn't get left behind. But who decided that verbal communication is more valuable than other forms of expression in the first place?[24] It's very possible that the loudness of those who prefer to speak overrides the preferences of the quieter part of the group. And let's not forget that 50 per cent of us are introverts, so if we feel that we're in the minority that's only because the others are louder![25] Say that a group meets to discuss whether to set up a new IT team in Berlin or Madrid. If the opinion being voiced first is that Berlin is better because that city has a large tech-savvy population, this becomes the point the discussion focuses on, and which gets most airtime. If objections are raised, they will usually be in relation to this point; that is, someone might say they don't think that Berlin has a higher level of IT skills. In the process, it becomes harder for other topics to be given attention and the conversation will naturally then focus on the comparison of IT skills, which narrows the scope of the discussion.

Often, quiet leaders reflect on what's being said by others instead of talking themselves.[26] They might feel that talking for the sake of talking is pointless and prefer to provide a contribution that's more thought-through than just sharing an opinion. Once they've considered what others have said, they'll provide a view which often goes beyond what the rest of the group have so far thought about. So far so good. However, quiet leaders who do this sometimes connect the dots in a way the rest of the group doesn't yet quite understand. This is detrimental to the introvert, who'll be seen as not quite 'getting it' when in reality they're slightly ahead of the rest of the group.[27] To avoid this perception, and bring the group along in the thought process, the introverted leader can say things like 'Let me go back to what was said a few moments ago. . .', '. . . this means that. . .', and '. . . taking this to its logical conclusion', or '. . . if we combine this with what was said earlier. . .'. This will help others to more easily see the connections, downstream impacts and consequences that are so obvious to the reflective introvert.

The more successful introverted leaders ignore the advice to get their voice heard early in a meeting and instead work on bringing others in the group along with their thought process. They get comfortable with who they are and use their strengths instead of attempting to play the meeting game with extroverted strengths such as early talking and 'loudness' of voice. They're true to themselves and know that this adds value to the organisation – they're quietly confident. Ignoring the primacy effect doesn't make it any less real, and it may mean that the quiet leader has to be creative in how to bring others along; for example, by following up individually after a meeting, or thinking ahead to how the discussion might unfold to be prepared for how to best persuade along the course of action (or no action) they believe is right. This sounds like more work, but means the quiet leader can relax and be themselves – and the good news is doing this prep work comes naturally to the quiet leader anyway and is probably something they would do ahead of each meeting in any case![28]

- **Anchoring effect:** Studies show that, in situations where there are a lot of unknowns and we have limited background information, we're more likely to let others guide us. This applies whether we're an expert in the field or not.[29] Our decisions can therefore be more influenced by others than we'd like to think. If you're about to place an offer on an eBay item that's listed with a start price of £1 and which accepts offers, your offer is likely to be near to the £1 – the start price creates an 'anchor' and your offer is more likely to be nearer this value than if there was no pre-set amount; you're not placing an offer based on what the item is objectively worth. Similarly, a study showed that students with prior high marks are more likely to receive higher marks in future, as the prior grades are being used by the assessor as a benchmark and starting point.[30]

Interestingly, this anchoring effect also works even when the value has nothing to do with the decision we're about to make. An experiment performed by Amos Tversky showed that even when we spin a wheel of fortune that gives out random numbers, and we're then subsequently asked to state how many member countries there are in the United Nations, the wheel of fortune number influences the response. The wheel creates an anchor that affects our answers even when that number is random.[31]

This means that, similar to the primacy effect, those who introduce an anchor earlier in a conversation are more likely to have a higher degree of influence of the direction of the discussion and the decision being made unless the group leader and others are aware of this tendency and can counteract it.

- **In- and out-group bias:** We feel safer when we have some certainty about our environment, and that includes the behaviours of those around us. To create certainty, we assume that people who are similar to us will come to similar conclusions and behave in ways similar to ourselves, and there's therefore comfort in having those people around us. It takes less energy this way and it's generally easier to deal with others who see the world in the same way we do. We see this as a good thing because it creates less emotional disruption to us as individuals; however, what's easier for us individually isn't in our organisations' best interests. Groups of people who think in similar ways have the same blind spots. I cover this in more detail in Chapter 4, but for now suffice to say that people who we consider similar to us are the 'in-group' and those who are different in some way are the 'out-group'. Who's 'in' and who's 'out' can be based on anything – ethnicity, gender, socio-economic background, personality, hairstyle, favourite football team, whether you drink alcohol or not, nationality, religion or your sense of humour. It really can be anything that differentiates you from the rest of the group, and the sad truth is we're more likely to listen to those we consider to be 'in' group even if we don't know that we're dividing those around us into these two groups. The groupings can often be arbitrary; someone can be of a different religion and gender to you and still be considered 'in-group' if, for instance, you went to the same university.[32]

Anyone who's good at making quick social connections (however superficial), such as extroverts, has a slight head start because they're more likely to find overlapping areas of common ground and therefore be considered in other people's in-groups at work.

- **Confirmation bias:** We've already seen that we make assumptions about how an introvert behaves. Because we have these assumptions, we expect to see these behaviours, and in turn, because we expect to see them, they're easier for us to spot when they occur. This is the essence of confirmation bias – we more easily see what we expect to see and gloss over the evidence that goes against the perception we already hold. For instance, there's a bias that women are more nurturing than men, and if you believe this you're more likely to see evidence of it than men behaving in a nurturing way. When James Bond actor Daniel Craig carried his infant child in public, it was more likely to be seen as an exception, and celebrated or ridiculed depending on your point of view.[33] Similarly, if you're an Asian man you're more likely to be stereotyped as less assertive than your white counterparts, and we're therefore more likely to pay attention when you're **not** acting in an assertive manner.[34]

Being led by confirmation bias has obvious dangers, one of which is that we don't actually see people as they are, we see them only through the lens of our assumptions about them.

- **Halo effect:** Where we have a positive view of someone due
to their actions in one sphere and they're assumed to also be
competent in another, completely separate, area. We often
see that technically competent individuals are promoted to
manager positions even though their technical ability is a
completely separate set of skills; it's assumed that their technical
skills translate to the skills required of a manager.[35]

  Extroverts are more likely to benefit from this bias because
they're generally more vocal, and therefore others – in combination with the action bias and primacy effect – are more likely to
over-inflate the importance of the extrovert's contribution to a
project.

- **Dominant behaviour bias:** Research has shown that we stop
thinking for ourselves – that we actually have less brain activity –
when someone behaves in a dominant way towards us, that
is they're brash, assertive, perhaps even aggressive or dismissive.
According to Stephen Martin and Joseph Marks in *Messengers:
Who We Listen To, Why We Don't, And Why*, this stems from our
primate days when social dominance, such as loudness and
certainty, served as a way to 'encourage hierarchical co-operation'
and thereby help us avoid the 'unnecessary and repeated cost of
conflict'.[36] We conflate dominance with competence and skill,
and give social status to the person displaying these behaviours.
We assume dominant individuals are people we should look
to for guidance, that they make better decisions than us. This
is confidence misunderstood through an extroverted lens.[37]
Self-aggrandising confidence isn't competence; just because
someone makes a statement with conviction doesn't mean that
the statement is true. Sometimes confidence is actually someone
who is 'confidence-appearing' – a confidence that's superficial
and attention-seeking – and this can be difficult to separate from
hubris.[38] True inner confidence doesn't need to be loud, but our
brains aren't always able to understand that and we're drawn
in, not thinking rationally. I used to work with someone who
was always critical of others – he was so vocal and negative that

everyone was worried that they'd be his next target, and therefore did whatever they could to be in his good books. Whenever he criticised an initiative, others didn't speak up because they didn't want to be on his radar. In this way, he used dominance to take control in the social hierarchy.

This inaccurate conferring of high social status from dominant behaviours would be more acceptable if it didn't have such profound implications for introverts in the workplace. Let me give another example. An audit manager called Sarah discussed team performance with a new colleague (in this organisation all managers had to compare their own team's performance assessments to ensure that no one was being stricter or more lenient with the rating scale than others, and ratings were consistent across the region). Sarah went through her performance ratings for her London team and the colleague, Maeve, expressed surprise when they got to two particular VPs, one high in extroversion and the other on introversion. They were both good performers in their own way, but Maeve had assumed that the extrovert was the higher performer, as she'd been using his own statements as a reference point. When he'd said 'I'm so busy', 'This is such a complex piece of work' or 'I introduced this new metric', she'd taken him at his word. From Sarah's perspective as his line manager, however, 'I'm so busy' was due to him spending a lot of time in the kitchen talking to co-workers; 'this is so complex' was because he didn't have the relevant experience to do it more quickly; and 'I introduced this' came from a team discussion where many individuals contributed. The introvert was the more technically skilled and stronger performer, but had made no equivalent statements; they'd just get on with delivering good work, which led Maeve to think they were adequate but nothing special. When the performance rating Sarah gave to the extrovert didn't reflect Maeve's expectations, she realised she only had his self-referencing statements to base her judgement on.

It's unfortunate that we're letting ourselves be fooled as it means organisations all over the world see style over substance, conflating confidence for competence, and losing out on great talent as a result.[39]

- **The Dunning–Krueger effect:** Someone of low competence is more likely to consider themselves an expert than a genuine expert would. This happens because the genuine expert is well aware of their gaps in knowledge, whereas the amateur believes they have the complete picture and doesn't know better.[40] We're notoriously bad at identifying whether someone is certain of something because they know what they're talking about, or just confident-sounding, and we therefore confuse certainty and confidence with competence. In today's complex business environment this is particularly unfortunate because it's increasingly difficult to state – in the moment or afterwards – that any individual is definitely wrong; it's usually always possible to identify one or more other factors that could also have contributed, and this gives the Dunning–Krueger effect lots of room to flourish. This is particularly damaging for introverts who rarely speak up unless they're sure of the factual accuracy of what they're about to say, and who prefer to think through the complexities before making statements with conviction. Someone who cares less about accuracy won't be held back by this preference for accuracy. To counter this bias, it's again important to remember that certainty, conviction and confidence don't equal competence.

## You know what they say about assumptions

The biases we all have, as a result of millions of years of evolution, once helped us as a species to survive but are no longer fit for purpose. Using mental shortcuts is human, so we all do it – but it's important that we initiate the slower-thinking part of our brain to override the initial default. We'd all like to think that we're autonomous beings and that we make all our decisions independently and consciously, without undue influence from others. This chapter has shown that that's unrealistic, and if you don't think you've got blind spots, you're actually more likely to be driven by your amygdala than someone who's more alert to its dangers!

Regardless of whether the bias is coming from ourselves or those around us, the perceptions we hold drive the decisions we make. The expression 'perception is reality' isn't true – it's our reality, but a perception we hold doesn't show us how *they* really are, just how *we* are, through our biases and the assumptions we make – but if we're driven by our assumptions our perceptions still influence our actions. In a work context, that means the perception we have of someone will influence our behaviour towards that person regardless of whether this is based on fact or not, such as our input into their performance appraisal, the likelihood that we'll recommend them for a promotion, or just simply how likely we are to believe a rumour about them. If someone is behaving in a way that supports our bias, we're more likely to believe the perception, and this is particularly problematic for introverts. An introvert may be affected by the perception that they're not sufficiently action-oriented or decisive, and therefore seen less as solid leadership material.[41] Traditionally, introverts have been coached on this, been guided to be aware of the perception of introverts, and to change behaviours to not give any reasons for others to see them as the stereotype. This managing of perceptions, however, doesn't lead to introverts being our authentic leading selves, doesn't allow us to bring our whole personalities forward, and doesn't give the organisation the full benefit of the introverted skillset. What we instead need to do is to bring into the light that this extroverted default exists, showcase the skills introverts bring to the table by putting quiet leadership skills further to front of mind when we think about what good looks like and generate a higher level of awareness of the connection between these skills and organisational high performance.

So, let's explore how we can go about making this shift. Who decides what good leadership looks like and how can we influence the changes in perception needed to improve organisational performance and get the best out of everyone we work with? We're not as good at recognising good leadership as we think we are, but could it be that the breadcrumbs we need to create a more complete picture are already there, and that all we need to do is connect some dots?

# A section for self-reflection

- - - - - - - - - - - - - - - - - - - - - - - - - - - - - - - - - - - - - -

- Which colleagues do you get along with best? Why do you think this is?

- Which heuristics do you use, and what is it about your environment that drives you to leverage those?

- What daily steps can you take to look out for mental shortcuts?

- - - - - - - - - - - - - - - - - - - - - - - - - - - - - - - - - - - - - -

# chapter 3

---

# What types of leaders do we want and need?

When we think of a 'leader' our minds usually create an image of a tall, smiling, confident and usually white male dressed in a crisp, perfectly fitted suit in front of a large crowd and wowing them with his charisma and charm. This image is generated from the stereotypes we talked about in Chapter 2 and is based on our biases, assumptions and perceptions; it doesn't necessarily mean this is a true good leader. Instead of relying on biases, let's delve into what decades of research and thought leadership tell us about how a good leader behaves. I'll build on Chapters 1 and 2 by expanding on the introvert as a leader, and compare the skills that quiet leaders bring to the table with skills that management and leadership literature say we need. Unfortunately, it turns out we're not very good at identifying good leadership traits,[1] and there's a big difference between what we say we want in our leaders and the behaviours we actually encourage.

# The core of the quiet leader

In Chapter 1 I shared that there are both biological and environmental reasons for why someone has a preference for introversion. From the neurological, sociological and psychological studies completed predominantly from the early 2000s to today,[2] we know there are certain traits more often found in introverts than in extroverts. Reviewing these resources, we find that there's a set of core quiet leadership behaviours that the introvert finds easier to access, largely as a result of their preference for reflection in solitude and thinking before speaking.[3] The list of skills they identify is not insubstantial. Can you have a think about which skills they might be?

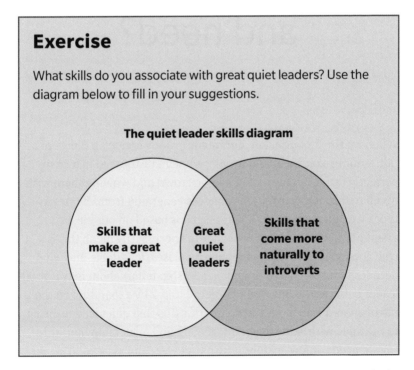

## Exercise

What skills do you associate with great quiet leaders? Use the diagram below to fill in your suggestions.

**The quiet leader skills diagram**

Skills that make a great leader

Great quiet leaders

Skills that come more naturally to introverts

The list of quiet leadership skills can be grouped into the following high-level areas listed in the box below. Do they match the list you created?

## A selection of quiet leadership skills key today

- Humility
- Listening
- Observing
- Self-awareness
- Being reflective and able to 'connect the dots'
- Having empathy
- Staying calm and in control of own emotions

Each of the qualities in the list above come more naturally to the quiet leader than the extrovert and are all key in today's corporate world. Although not an exhaustive list of all leadership skills (and there are too many skills required of a leader for any single individual to have all of them), it contains crucial skills for enhanced performance.[4] Introverts will benefit from taking more ownership and being proud of these skills which they're more easily able to access, and extroverts will benefit too if they leverage the quiet leader's arsenal.

## Quiet charisma

The list of skills above is a quiet list – it's a list that showcases certain types of talents and traits over others, and they're low key by definition. Good leadership doesn't need to be loud and some solitude is necessary.[5] However, this isn't to say that we don't need leaders to be charismatic and vocal – being a leader in your field and not sharing your views and constantly being in solitude is no good to anyone.[6] Leadership needs interaction and connection, and as a leader you do need to make yourself heard. There are just different ways of going about this and some are just as – if not more – effective as the methods we might normally consider. Extroverts don't have a monopoly on charisma and being vocal. If we think introverts are unable to be these things, it's because we hold personal biases and make assumptions about what an introvert is (see Chapter 2). It's perfectly possible for introverts to be inspirational, high-energy and bringing people together towards a common goal. They might just do it differently to how an extrovert would.

Introverts can deliver rousing and emotional speeches, and inspire large audiences and persuade and win hearts and minds. Think of Martin Luther King, Jr's speech *I have a dream*, which was critical in accelerating the Civil Rights movement in the US and to this day evokes strong emotions as a clear and loud call to action. Or think of Neil Armstrong being selected as the first man on the moon; NASA decided that Armstrong was the best choice in part due to his quiet, calm and humble nature. They felt he would better represent the United States at this critical moment in history,[7] an early example of an understanding that sometimes quiet traits are more impactful, and – depending on how and when they're leveraged – can have just as strong, if not stronger, an emotional impact as the traditional loud personality-driven leadership style that we tend to consider to be 'charismatic'.

I mentioned in Chapter 1 that a key misunderstanding about introversion is that it's often conflated with shyness and low energy, which leads to the misconception that introverted individuals aren't able to give impassioned performances and emotional speeches, persuading others through charisma and charm. The many actors, musicians and other creatives who consider themselves to be introverts disprove this idea and show that being quiet is no obstacle to having charisma. This is a point worth reiterating to remind ourselves that leadership can be executed in many ways; loud doesn't equate to confident, and charisma and charm don't solely belong to extroverts.

## Exercise

In Chapter 1 I listed some of the actors, musicians and other creatives who consider themselves to be quiet. Can you think of other quiet, prominent individuals able to be charismatic in their own unique way and engage at an emotional level?

## A selection of quiet leaders with high emotional impact

Barack Obama
Neil Armstrong
Elon Musk
Abraham Lincoln
JK Rowling
Mahatma Ghandi
Mother Theresa
Ruth Bader Ginsberg
Angelina Jolie
Keanu Reeves
Emma Watson
Tom Hardy
Malala Yousafzai
Martin Luther King, Jr

# What does a good leader do?

What good looks like depends in part on what we need from our leader for the situation at hand. Therefore, to enhance performance we want to use the full buffet of skills available and not ignore or undervalue a large proportion of talent. Some leaders create a vision for others to follow, some develop people, some coach and support – and all are equally valuable. A list of key roles could look something like this:[8]

- Create a vision and target state for others to follow and work towards.
- Develop people, including coaching and support.
- Remove roadblocks and enabling their teams to execute.
- Inspire their teams to do better.
- Drive innovations and improvements.
- Set the standard for acceptable and unacceptable behaviours.

The same individual doesn't need to do all these things, but the leader's role is to make sure that the team collectively have the skills in place to support each other to perform at their best, and to ensure that the group dynamic works to the organisation's benefit.[9] The challenges are many in today's environment; the pace of technological advances, the prevalence of social media as a tool for influence and associated risk, increased human longevity, increased intergenerational interaction and confusion, to name a few challenges we've not had to this extent previously. All these elements create working environments that are more dynamic and potentially disruptive than in prior decades. The complexity this brings requires us to leverage all the different skills of today's leaders, including those of the quiet leader – and in many cases, the skills of the quiet leader are better suited (the technological shifts also create more opportunities for influence for the quiet leader as they have a wider range of options available to persuade others).

# Theories of leadership

Many leadership theorists have identified different ways of being a good leader, and there are many schools of thought. Rather than attempt an exhaustive list, which would take up a whole book on its own, let's see what these researchers say about the skills needed to be a good leader and compare it to the quiet leader's natural skillset. Would you be surprised if I say there's a large overlap?

Let's start with the theory of 'servant leadership', introduced by Robert K. Greenleaf in his 1970 essay *The leader as servant*. A servant leader prioritises the goals and objectives of the team above their own personal goals. This mirrors Simon Sinek's idea that 'leaders eat last', where the leader puts the well-being of the team ahead of themselves. In order to be this leader, you have to have empathy in order to understand your team and what they need, and you have to have good listening and observational skills to get to the core of what they truly need from you. Crucially, you also need to have the humility to be content with not always being in the limelight, and accept the risk that your team might outgrow you and become better than you.[10]

After the idea of servant leadership, the 'stewardship' concept gained ground, first introduced by Dr Robert Clifton in 1987. The concept of stewardship is similar to servant leadership in that it's based on the idea that the leader has responsibility for something greater than themselves, and focus on putting others first, primarily the organisation and through this their teams. Stewardship implies a longer time horizon, sometimes even multi-generational, and the leader is a temporary guardian of the organisation. Skills-wise, this approach requires much of the same of the leader as the servant model and draws on the same natural benefits from the introvert; that is, the humility to know that they're one in a chain of steward leaders of the organisation's future, and the self-awareness to know when to step back, as well as the listening and observational skills needed to understand when to take input from those around them.[11]

Going further back in time, to 1939, psychologist Kurt Lewin introduced the idea of 'democratic leadership', which highlights the importance of taking feedback from your team and involving them in decision-making. Doing this well means leveraging the quiet skills of active listening to hear from others, humility to ask for the input to begin with, and the calmness to respond appropriately and with curiosity regardless of what the input is.[12]

In 1973, sociologist James V. Daunton came up with the idea of 'transformational leadership', which encourages innovation and creativity, and to make the team feel heard and valued. A core pillar of the transformational leadership concept is to listen to the team. Therefore, transformational leaders need to show high levels of genuine listening and have high levels of empathy.[13]

In recent years there's also been a wave of 'radical candor', developed by Kim Scott, a framework for caring enough about your team to give direct and helpful feedback without sugar-coating the message. The idea is that this will ultimately be more helpful for them over the course of their careers, although possibly harder in the moment. It might be counterintuitive that an introvert could be successful at this because we often think of introverts as conflict averse. Partly this stems from the bias we talked about in Chapter 2 and reflects a view we might hold ourselves that giving negative feedback equates to conflict, but the empathetic introvert instead sees this as a way to help their team and not as conflict per se. Engaging with negative messages comes from a place of genuinely wanting to see the team succeed. The quiet leader has a higher-than-average ability to observe and therefore understands real-time how the feedback is received and can adjust accordingly, while at the same time calmly engaging in the dialogue and handling any negative emotions that arise.[14]

Beyond this, management theorists from Henri Fayol (*The 14 Principles of Management*) to Peter Drucker (*Practice of Management*) have highlighted the importance of analysis and forward planning on a person's ability to succeed as a leader, which we know are key introverted skills. Theorists on interpersonal and business relationships from Dale Carnegie (*How to Win Friends and Influence People*) via James C. Collins (*Good to Great*) to Patrick Lencioni (*Five Dysfunctions of a Team*) have emphasised how humility and empathy are powerful leadership attributes, and again also key quiet leadership skills.[15]

This is a small selection of original leadership ideas and concepts, and many more have been based on the ideas outlined above and sometimes developed further, all of which show that being a good leader very often overlaps with the skills of the quiet leader.

# The quiet leader's advantage

We can safely say that introverts naturally possess skills that give them the potential to be great leaders, and those with a behavioural preference for introversion have an advantage in today's complex world where an increasing number of decisions are less clear-cut than they might have been in the past. This isn't to say that introverts always make better leaders than extroverts – I've seen several introverted individuals in leadership positions who should never have been there – and in any case introversion and extroversion is only one element that goes into making someone a good leader (also relevant are elements such as work experience, organisational culture and being willing to set aside the time to develop and being conscious about your leadership method). But it does mean there are a number of key leadership skills that introverts possess and which come more easily to them than to an extrovert. This is a key point to make as I want to be clear I'm not attempting to sideline extrovert leaders or minimise the benefits of what they add. What we need to do, however, is to start to recognise that extroverted behaviours are not the only leadership behaviours we want and need, to understand that extroverted leadership behaviours have downsides, and that quiet leadership may be more appropriate and generate better results in many situations in today's corporate and organisational environment. There's room for different types of leaders, and what works in one context might not work in another; there's no one size fits all. There are situations where an extrovert is better than an introvert; for example, research has shown that we gravitate towards those who show certainty whenever times are uncertain (and extroverts are more likely to be in this category). This could be if we're in a location affected by war or unrest, or if there are threats of redundancies where we work. Similarly, there are instances where an introvert is better: For instance, if a situation is highly complex and new, or if you're a proactive and highly educated employee, in which case you're more likely to perform better under an introverted leader.[16]

There's no rule that says one approach is better than the other, but we have an imbalance between the two skillsets in current discourse. We should recognise the weaknesses of the extrovert more and shine a stronger light on the strengths of the introvert. Leveraging the skills from both groups will benefit everyone. If we can all value each other's contributions more, we may also more readily be willing to choose the behaviours that fit the outcome we need in the best possible way, while staying true to our own personalities and selves, which we'll explore more in Chapter 5.

## What we have vs what we need

Quiet skills are valuable for good leadership, and yet we don't see this translate into practice in most workplaces. The introvert's contribution isn't sufficiently recognised – in fact it's far too often the opposite, that quiet individuals find themselves side-lined, not given enough credit and aren't progressing as quickly as their extroverted counterparts. This is to the detriment of their teams, their organisations and to the introverts themselves. On the one hand, we're told that leaders should be humble, but they should also have the courage of their convictions; we're told leaders need to listen more, and yet those who are the most vocal get access to more opportunities; leaders need to take care of their teams, but self-promoters are more often recognised. There are two main reasons for this. Firstly, our organisations haven't always evolved from the approaches developed during the industrial revolution, designed to standardise and improve efficiency rather than leveraging each employee's unique skills for enhanced performance, and developed at a time when most work was physical and repetitive.[17] At the time, we were in environments where only a small proportion were educated to degree level, most people trusted authority and those around us were mostly similar to ourselves – additionally, there was no Google or open source research databases where it was possible for everyone to educate themselves sufficiently to challenge the establishment as rapidly as we can today. There were counter-cultures of course, but they were largely on the fringes, not yet fully established and usually not well coordinated. There are pockets of leaders who want to do things differently today, but it's not easy to make drastic cultural changes in organisations where old behaviours are well entrenched in frameworks, policies and expectations.

Secondly, the extrovert default with its underlying biases (see Chapter 2) is still hugely prevalent as the default expectation even if we know intellectually that introverted skills are beneficial.[18] As Marquet states in *Turn the Ship Around!* it's hard to give up the traditional personality-driven leader-follower model,[19] just as it's hard to engage with our biases and assumptions. Both require effort and energy and takes work at a personal level as well as an organisational one. Changing how we view leadership requires us to move away from our current overemphasis on self-promotion and visibility, towards a genuine focus on sustainable delivery, reviewing actual long-term organisational results and focusing on the psychological safety of individuals – it requires looking at actual results objectively, and to stop talking in order to hear good ideas from more sources.

Counteracting our biases of what a good leader is will become even harder and require more self-awareness at all levels as technology continues to evolve and we increase the use of artificial intelligence (AI). Consider these examples: An AI tool created by online news source BuzzFeed in July of 2023 generated a set of 'national Barbies' to support the launch of the international hit film *Barbie*. These weren't Barbie dolls in real life to be sold by Mattell, just AI-generated images intended to show a representative view of women in various countries. The results of the 195 countries included a South Sudan Barbie with a rifle, a Lebanese Barbie standing on rubble, and almost all Barbies with white skin and facial features regardless of which country they represented (the article has since been removed).[20] Similarly, if you Googled 'CEO' a couple of years ago, the majority of images you'd see would show a white male. Back in 2015, Google would show a gorilla when searching for a 'black man'. As of middle of 2023, this was 'fixed' only through a manual workaround involving the removal of photos of gorillas from their inventory in this search,[21] and in early 2024 the bias problem became even clearer when historical figures such as Nazis were all exclusively non-white – to put it mildly, it's extremely unlikely there were Asian members of the SS, and we know there weren't any African American US presidents before 2008.[22] These examples all show how technology perpetuates and reinforces our biases through the datasets and coding that the AI models are trained on. The images of South Sudanese Barbies with rifles don't tell us anything more about women in South Sudan any more than a white male CEO tells us about good leadership. In the quiet leader context, this exemplifies that our biases run deep, and it's time we question our automatic defaults and take a close look at the behaviours we promote in our organisations, consciously or unconsciously. The quiet leader biases won't show up in a Google image search very easily, but still perpetuate our view of what a good leader is.

Let me give an example of how assumptions can affect perceptions of leadership, from one of the discussions I had with quiet leaders during the research for this book: Lisa is a senior director in a global financial services institution based in the UK. She recently had two senior team members – one introvert and one extrovert – who were both capable performers, with equal years of relevant work experience. The introvert had been doing this particular role for several years longer than the extrovert and the quality and experience was reflected in their higher performance rating. This difference in performance wasn't always so clear to others on the outside, however, and the next time a larger role came up that suited both of their skillset, the extrovert ended up being offered the role over Lisa's objections. As their manager, she knew there was difference in performance, but the hiring manager ignored the objective measure of the performance rating and instead went with their 'gut feel' that the extrovert would be the better candidate. They relied on their assumptions and were led by the oversimplified thinking that there's such a thing as a 'natural leader' and that this is represented by extroverted traits.

This is the same situation that quiet leaders often find themselves in; assumptions are being made about their capabilities and contributions because they behave differently to the extrovert leaders we see and hear more often. As we noted in Chapter 2, however, we see these behaviours more often because of the biases we all have, not because there are more people with these traits or they're better leaders – after all, about 40 per cent of all US executives are introverts, so we know that the more quiet individuals do have a place in the leadership chair and should be proud of what they add to their organisations without having to adjust their behaviours materially.[23] With the challenges we face in today's globalised and fast-paced environment, with rapidly changing technology, and where we work with a wide range of personalities, our organisations and our colleagues will all benefit if we expand our view of what leadership looks like beyond the historical default. Now more than ever it's important that we leverage and reinforce all positive leadership behaviours, and give increased emphasis to what the quiet leader adds.

## The next stage

Good leadership is whatever we collectively define it to be and what we encourage in practice, and so it's possible to change and expand our view of what good looks like, to include what the leadership theorists are telling us good should look like, and to improve our own leadership styles in the process. It's still too easy to fool the decision-makers, and 'selling yourself' is still too large a part of our ability to progress. This is why we need to improve leadership at all levels, and examine and challenge the assumptions we hold. If we're able to do this, we'll be rewarded with higher-performing teams, we'll leverage the strengths of a wider range of people and we'll stop wasting so much talent. We know we have the tools available to achieve this, and we know that there's a high correlation between a quiet leader's behaviour and high performance – even though this isn't yet recognised in most organisations. With a quiet leader's skillset fitting in well with what leading leadership theorists advocate for, and have done for some time, we can say clearly that introverts do indeed make good leaders.

So what do we need to do to change the default images that appear in our minds when we think of a 'leader', and convert what we know about the benefits of introverted strengths to a more inclusive approach that appreciates and recognises these skills in practice? We have started doing it with gender and race, and slowly too with neurodivergence. We now need to expand our diversity thinking to a wider range of categories such as personality traits, and elevate leadership across the board.

# A section for self-reflection

- What kind of leadership style do you leverage most often? Why do you think this is?
- Who's the best leader you've ever worked with? What made them so impressive?
- What traits do you value in your leaders, and how do these overlap with quiet skills?
- Who's listened to in your organisation? What factors do you think drive this?

# chapter 4

---

# Creating successful and diverse teams

We saw in Chapter 3 that what we think we want in a good leader doesn't always align with what we seek out in practice. Tackling the mental shortcuts we mentioned in Chapter 2 is a key way to fix this issue and enhance the likelihood that we get the leaders we say we want. Another issue which should be tackled in parallel and which is related is to increase the pool from which those leaders are selected. Diversity, equity and inclusion (DEI) has had a major increase in importance (at least optically) over the last few years, with many organisations now hiring Chief Diversity Officers as part of their C-suite and Boards, and more considerations are being made around how we create high-performing teams, and which population we draw on when we consider who our leaders should be. The nature of personality should also form part of this relatively new body of research, but is not yet fully integrated, so in this chapter I'll focus more on the interaction between DEI work and introversion, and how expanding our view of what a good leader looks like also supports the wider DEI movement.

# What do you mean?

Given the complexity of the DEI topic, and the often-emotional discussions associated with it, it's especially important that we're clear on what we mean with each term before we continue. DEI concepts often have different meanings ascribed to them even among individuals involved directly with DEI work. To avoid confusion, and to prevent us getting diverted from the real conversation, I've outlined below how the terms will be used here, exemplified with my own version of a popular shoe analogy that you might have come across before.[1]

- **Diversity:** Bringing variety to an organisation and having lots of different types of people around – if we're in a shoe shop, this means having lots of different types of shoes; trainers, flip flops, high heels, clogs, the list goes on.

- **Equity and equality:** Equity is where the same outcome is achieved for individuals regardless of their starting point. In shoe terms, the store has enough shoes in different sizes to ensure everyone gets a pair that fits. This differs from equality in that equity focuses on fairness of **outcomes** (everyone gets a pair that fits), whereas equality focuses on fairness of opportunity (everyone can enter the shop and there's enough shoes for everyone). Equity – focus on outcomes – sounds good in theory, but there's a downside we need to be aware of: It might create a sense of unfairness for some (to push the analogy, those with short feet might be frustrated that those with longer feet use more fabric to make their shoes). Similarly, a downside of equality (everyone has the same starting point) is that the bias we saw in Chapter 2 will likely be a factor; even though the theory is that everyone gets a shoe, the allocation of shoes might not be fair and free of bias. In corporate environments, this means that someone who's introverted gets an opportunity to interview for a role, but the unconscious biases of the interviewers mean they don't give the role to the quiet leader because they – unknowingly – assess the quiet candidate differently and apply assumptions to their capabilities. Despite this, it *looks* as if there's equality of opportunity, and now it's the introvert's fault that they didn't get the role, perpetuating the damage.

- **Inclusion:** Where employees feel safe to be themselves, bring their 'best selves' to work, and can leverage their unique skills as much as possible – or, in other words, everyone feels free to wear the shoes they want.

The goal is that these elements together lead to a sense of belonging and safety, as shown in Figure 4.1, enabling everyone to contribute with their own unique set of skills. Do you feel you have all components in your current organisation? If not, is there anything you can personally do about this or is the issue structural?

Note that 'being yourself' at work doesn't mean 'bring absolutely all of yourself, including the bad bits' – it's still a professional environment – but we should aspire to an environment where it feels acceptable to show your individual skills, and to relax enough to contribute with your unique perspective. This leads to higher-performing individuals and to a higher-performing organisation.[2]

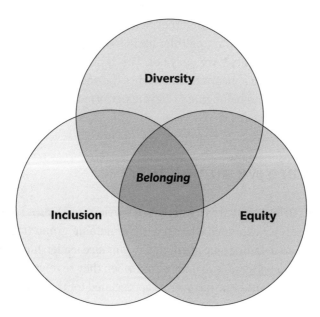

**Figure 4.1** Belonging and safety are key for individuals to thrive

Those who aren't in the 'default' we referred to in Chapter 2 will know what I mean when I say there's pressure on how to behave when you're not in the standard 'in-group'. Therefore, what we're aiming for is to take away the pressure to be like a particular group or type and be recognised for the contributions you uniquely make. On this note, there is one point to highlight: When talking about diversity, you might hear the expression diversity of **thought**, which is intended to reflect that diversity goes beyond the traditional areas of race, religion and gender, and also covers broader topics such as socio-economic background, neurodivergence and – this book argues – neurological differences such as introversion and extroversion. We need to be mindful when we push for diversity of thought that we don't just select one category of diversity that we find easier to achieve, set a target, proceed to meet that target and then consider it mission accomplished – this wouldn't be true progress. I once interviewed a group of senior managing directors who proudly stated that theirs was a diverse organisation because their employees came from a range of different universities. I looked around the room and they were nearly all white, middle-aged men. Perhaps it's accurate that they had some diversity of thought because some were from wealthier backgrounds than others, but is that genuine diversity? Arguably not. This is one of the reasons why diversity has to be a means to an end, not the end state – the goal has to be inclusion and belonging to elevate performance, not diversity to tick a box.

## What are we aiming for?

I'd like us to work towards a removal of barriers and biases so there's true fairness for everyone who's not in the 'default' group (indeed there'd be no default group at all) and to enhance leadership so that managers are better able to understand when they're relying on biases. In that world, the introvert is appreciated for their unique and valuable skills just as much as the louder extrovert. Not better or worse, just different. You may have seen a visual for this idea already –

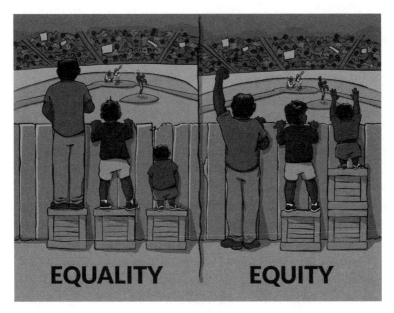

**Figure 4.2** Equity and equality mindsets produce different actions and outcomes, but what we ultimately need is to remove the systemic barriers that hold us back

Credit: Interaction Institute for Social Change

I've included one below in Figure 4.2, with three people standing in front of a fence trying to watch a baseball game, but only one person is tall enough to see over the fence and catch what's going on in the game.[3] The shortest person is given a box to stand on (the equivalent of getting a shoe that fits from the shoe example above) so they're now all able to see. What we're aiming for, however, is to have no fence at all. If the fence (our biases and assumptions, micro-aggressions and unintended consequences of initiatives) were removed, they'd all be able to see the game without the shortest person needing the box. What we should be doing isn't to focus our efforts on determining who gets a box, how many boxes, or the size or shape of the box, but instead we should be working towards removing the fence altogether – organisationally, this means creating a culture where everyone (introverts included) is recognised for the contributions they bring, and we have a clearer picture of the weaknesses of extroverts so that there's more balance between the two. This would mean we could use the unique capabilities of each group better than we do today. (This isn't to say the introvert doesn't also have weaknesses; however, most organisations already focus too much on these so no further emphasis is needed.)

And, unfortunately, it may not be obvious to everyone that the introvert's skillset isn't fully leveraged today. As you know from Chapter 2, when we can't observe something, we have a tendency to assume there's nothing there. In *Introvert Power,* Helgoe uses the image of a military aide and a General to show this: If we don't see the general on the battlefield we assume they're not there. The extrovert has the General on the outside, very clearly present. In other words, it's very obvious what the extrovert is thinking and what decision they've reached the minute they've reached it. This isn't the case with introverts, who keep their cards closer to their chest to begin with – their General is actually on the inside and we only see the aide on the outside. Extroverts assume that the introvert operates in the same way as them and mistakenly assume there's no General at all – they think the introvert is meek and indecisive, which wouldn't make them suitable leadership material.[4] And this is where we're going wrong: We've always been told we should do unto others as we'd like to have done unto us (to follow the golden rule), but that's what the extroverts are doing when they assume that introverts behave exactly like them. We need to instead adopt the *platinum rule*, do unto others as *they* would like to have done unto them. In other words, let's start to see the introvert and their strengths for what they are, not through the eyes of the extrovert but as leaders in their own right. Let's stop assuming that there's nothing below the surface or that introverts have no General. The General is there, you just need to look.

## Diversity in action

In the DEI steering groups I've led and participated in over the course of my career, I've often seen that organisations have a desire to tackle one 'category' of diversity at a time, such as race first or gender first. The idea is to then move on to the next category, and the one after that, once the first category of inequity has been 'fixed'. This is well-intentioned and comes from wanting to give due attention to each minority. The approach, however, risks DEI becoming a series of 'initiatives' or projects, seen as time-bound by those within the organisation. Ultimately this doesn't lead to any changes in behaviour long term. For introverts, unfortunately, the approach is also likely to mean that our form of diversity wouldn't get tackled at all. Instead, what we need are organisations where people work actively and continuously to remove the barriers and assumptions, and on an ongoing basis strive for an environment where colleagues walk the walk and not just talk the talk. In other words, we're aiming for a permanent cultural shift, because the best teams flourish where there's an understanding of the strengths we each uniquely bring to the table, independently of the 'categories' we belong to. We all contribute based on our own individual mixture of categories such as race, gender, introversion/extroversion, experiences, socio-economic background, nationality, to name a few lenses that shape us.

Do you have ideas for how this could be achieved? Apart from simply improving management, some examples that others have come up with: An international insurance company with a focus on 'personal growth' to focus on the ability we all have to change our thinking and learn from our mistakes, which affects all forms of diversity and is more likely to make people aware of their biases and shift the culture longer term. Amazon employees set aside 20 minutes at the beginning of meetings to read the proposal to be discussed before the decision-making process starts. Their idea (developed by owner and CEO Jeff Bezos) is that this leads to better-informed discussion, bypassing the 'fast thinking' mechanism that so often leads to weaker decisions. Interestingly, introverts are more likely to read meeting papers beforehand anyway, but this approach helps the extroverts be better informed before speaking and not take the discussion in an unnecessary direction, saving everyone time. It could be argued that the Amazon approach is pandering to a lack of preparation, but at least this way the introvert doesn't need to waste time preparing if nobody else comes prepared. In a version of this, one leader I worked with made a point of stating to his executive team in every meeting that he assumed they'd read the content of the paper to be discussed already. Those who hadn't read the paper in advance the first time they heard this certainly made sure they had the next time around, reducing the number of 'silly questions' the presenters received before a decision could be reached or the recommended approach approved. Some are also starting to focus on understanding neurodivergent conditions: A global investment bank leads the field in this space, establishing a neurodiversity group for employees in the UK. In 2023, I worked with this group to add introversion to its scope and becoming even more inclusive (to be clear, introversion is not a neuro**divergency**, but we all process information differently and have different behavioural preferences, creating neuro**diversity**). Some of the actions this group took included setting up an Introversion Network, sharing guidance on how to bring out the best in introverted colleagues and team members, as well as introducing 'this is me' stories that normalised senior leaders who self-label as introverts. This helps to eliminate some of the extrovert bias and the extrovert default we talked about in Chapters 2 and 3.

## The ripple effect

The best actions by leading organisations also benefit those outside the immediate target group. For instance, we know from research that brainstorming doesn't always produce the best results, and we know that a lot of people – not limited to, but including introverts – find it hard to concentrate in an open office environment due to the noise generated from the conversations of others and general office noise.[5] To tackle this, a UK financial services institution in late 2023 put up posters around their offices to show employees which parts of their building were hotter/colder and louder/

quieter, to accommodate for personal preference and the types of work the employee needed to do that day. This knowledge-sharing equips employees with the information they need to make decisions for themselves to be as efficient and effective as possible. Accommodating different preferences like these, and introducing small changes to enable different types of employees to operate at their best, drives a higher level of productivity for the organisation. It may have been intended for a neurodiverse group, but benefitted everyone.

Alex, a director in a global 'Big 4' consultancy firm and one of the leaders I talked to as part of the research for this book, told me it could be a challenge to be an introvert in consulting, where large parts of your day – and your career success – are based on interaction with others. He told me about a leader who'd given him the courage to be himself as a quiet individual in the absence of many quiet role models in his industry: A senior partner shared a key detail about a personal struggle when not many others had opened up in the same way. The organisation's response to the colleague's personal disclosure showed Alex that he was in an organisation where it would be completely acceptable to be himself, even if there weren't many others like him who'd done the same. After some time in industry, away from consultancy, he came back to his Big 4 firm because that's where he could be himself the most, introversion and all. Encouraging openness and not hiding what you uniquely bring to the table can have benefits not just for yourself, but also benefit others who look up to you.

## The potential benefits

The benefits when we get it right can be substantial. But what happens when we don't? The following anecdote from Atul Gawande's book *The Checklist Manifestos* is an example of where the lack of diversity could have had deadly consequences.[6] A patient came to a hospital in San Francisco with bleeding from their abdomen, the result of a knife assault downtown. The doctors did their standard checks, they'd seen this a number of times before, and started to go through their procedures for stopping the bleeding, knowing they would have to get him to the operating theatre but feeling there was no immediate rush. But, suddenly, a nurse noticed that the patient had stopped talking. They checked his heart rate and it was through the roof. They tried everything – pushing air through his lungs, giving a blood transfusion, following all their standard processes. Except none of them worked so they went to surgery and blood came pouring out of his stomach. It turned out the knife had gone further in than they thought, into the aorta and directly by the heart. They put pressure on the artery and that stopped the worst of the bleeding, but how did a knife get that far in, in the first place? What hadn't occurred to anyone in the trauma team or any of the medical professionals who had seen this patient that day was that he had been attacked, not with a regular knife, as everyone had assumed from a street fight, but with . . . a bayonet.

This story was used in a book about the life-saving benefits of checklists, but it also tells us something useful about applying different perspectives. Nobody in that emergency room thought about bayonets – after all, they were in San Francisco where bayonets aren't a frequent sight. But who's to say that someone else with a different background – perhaps someone who performs historical re-enactments in their spare time – wouldn't have seen the potential for a different type of knife sooner than the original team members did. This is the true benefit of diversity of all kinds; everyone adds something different based on their own background, life experiences and genetic makeup, and unique skills. This is beneficial for organisations too: We know that a single leader can't have all the answers to every single problem the organisation is ever going to face. The idea of the 'lone genius' is simply not accurate – Thomas Edison was surrounded by engineers and other scientists when they through trial and error developed the light bulb, and Charles Darwin relied on botanists, zoologists and geologists to develop the theory of evolution.[7] Similarly, we know that companies benefit when we expand who we listen to and we capture a larger set of ideas in decision-making. Indeed, a Gallup Institute survey of over a million employees showed that being able to bring the best version of themselves to the job led to an increase in energy and willingness to learn,[8] key ingredients for being willing to go the extra mile and build high-performing teams.

With a wider range of traits in the team, it's more likely that different lenses and perspectives will be considered, as well as the organisation better representing the communities they're part of. Just like employees differ in working preferences, introverts and extroverts in leadership positions are equipped with different sets of qualities that are all needed.

Although individuals need to do the work, it shouldn't be up to individuals to take on this effort alone; we need systemic changes that recognise the value brought to the table by both introverts and extroverts in equal measure. This requires giving more emphasis to quiet leadership skills and shining a light on what might not be immediately obvious to the extrovert, and repeatedly reiterating the connection between introversion and good leadership skills so that everyone in the organisation can benefit and improve. Reaching our end goal also requires structures in place to ensure that the cultural shift is happening in practice. Personally, I'm a big fan of tangible actions that introduce an expectation of diversity into an existing process or procedure so that the more inclusive approach becomes the default, in essence *leveraging* our tendency towards biases. Amy Cuddy calls this 'choice architecture'. You might recognise it as the nudge concept I mentioned in Chapter 2. Human beings are influenced by both objective facts ('informational influence') as well as those around us ('normative influence'). [9] Because we're social beings, most of the time the normative influence weighs more heavily as we prefer to be part of the in-group.[10] Therefore, when we're making a decision we look first to see what the expectation is from those around us and in order to save on mental effort in determining the best course of action (those heuristics again), we usually choose the default. If it's clear what the standard process is, and this process drives diversity and inclusion, that option is more likely to be selected and it's also the one that gets us closer to the end goal. This talk about 'process' may seem boring to some, but as we'll see in the next chapter, behaviour that repeats time and time again will eventually become the behaviour that we go to automatically.

# A section for self-reflection

- - - - - - - - - - - - - - - - - - - - - - - - - - - - - - - - - - - -

- Are there situations you've been in recently where you might have been making assumptions about those around you and their thought processes? What was the outcome of those interactions?

- What types of diversity would you and your organisation find it easiest to 'meet target' for? Which ones would be more elusive?

- Do you often find yourself frustrated by those around you when they don't behave the way you expect them to? Where do you think those differences in behavioural expectations come from?

- - - - - - - - - - - - - - - - - - - - - - - - - - - - - - - - - - - -

# chapter 5

---

# How to flex your behaviour to any situation

So far, the focus of this book has been to increase emphasis on the quiet leader's strengths and the ways in which this can be achieved – and we've also talked about the performance benefits of creating a culture where everyone (introverts included) feels sufficiently safe and accepted enough to put their best selves forward. Part 2 will delve into the quiet leader's strengths and why they help drive enhanced performance, but before we get there I want to recognise that the quiet leader's strengths can be used by anyone. They're available to all, even though they're more easily accessible to the introvert. Therefore, before we segue to Part 2, let's take a brief look at the science of how anyone can benefit from the quiet leader's buffet of skills – also known as 'flexing' our behaviours.

# Building the muscle

You may have heard about the change curve, showing how we handle changes by first going through a stage of shock and denial, progressing to sadness, frustration and finally accepting the change (based on the Kubler-Ross model of the stages of grief that a terminal ill patient goes through when coming to terms with their own mortality).[1] This is often used as a basis for saying that most people aren't good at dealing with change, but in fact our brains are very good at it.[2] Over the last few decades, scientists have discovered something called neuroplasticity, which is a way of saying that our brains have the ability to re-wire themselves, learn and be moulded even in adulthood.[3] In fact, the neurons – the nerve cells that send messages around the brain and to our body – always take the shortest available route from point A to point B. What route they choose is learned and can therefore change with practice. For instance, it's been proven that individuals born blind who learn to read braille have more activity in the visual cortex, the brain region generally associated with processing images, indicating that this part of the brain learned to process the braille sensations instead of seeing images as it traditionally would.[4]

Although this is an extreme example, the same principle also applies to everyday scenarios. This means we can train our brain to learn new things and adopt new ways of behaving. If we put in the time to teach ourselves how to, the patterns of activity in the brain, as well as its very structure, can be changed away from the default developed based on our genes and experiences to date. The established psychological practice of cognitive behavioural therapy (CBT) has shown us that thoughts, actions and feelings are closely related, and that only one of the dimensions needs to change for the others to also adjust, as indicated by Figure 5.1.

Therefore, adopting a new behaviour can come about from introducing new ways of thinking (perhaps you've started this process yourself from reading this book) or from introducing and testing out new experiences. Interestingly, research also shows that

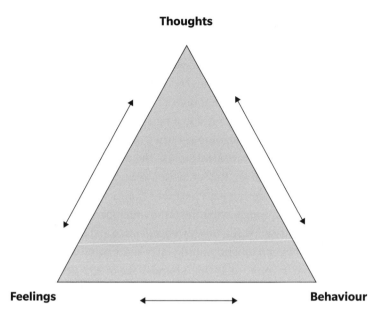

**Figure 5.1** To make changes, only one dimension (thoughts, feelings or behaviour) needs to change, and this will in turn affect the others

while nothing can quite beat doing the doing and practising a new behaviour in real life, it's surprisingly effective to just think about behaving in a new way. This too helps the brain practise the muscles needed to adapt to the new behaviour.[5]

Changing the way your brain is wired can't be done overnight. Stanford psychologist Carol Dweck notes in *Mindset* that changing your brain's auto-pilot is the opposite of surgery. In a surgery, the results are instant, like removing an appendix, whereas changing your brain's wiring needs practice and repeated exposure to the same behaviour (through thoughts and ideally actions) to make it more familiar.[6] The expression often used is 'neurons that fire together, wire together' to show that repetition is needed for a new, quicker route to be created in the brain and for new behaviours to stick longer term.

# You're still you

To begin with it might not feel like you're being yourself fully when you're trying out a new behaviour or action, and it might feel like you're not being authentic – that doesn't mean that you're 'faking it' and the behaviour isn't 'you', it just means that your neurons haven't fully created a new route yet (they're not taking the shortest one) and it's therefore more effort to use the new skill. This doesn't mean it'll feel fake forever. In fact, we all adapt already to varying degrees.[7] Think of meeting your partner's family for the first time; you'll automatically gauge what the family members are doing in order to identify what the unwritten rules are and adjust your own behaviour ever so slightly until you're more familiar with the new people in your life. Is this a handshake or a hugging kind of group? Until you know, you'll probably hold back a bit and either let your partner take the lead or wait until you're hugged by your future father-in-law before going in for a hug yourself. This isn't manipulative or not your authentic self, it's simply a way to understand how best to get along with those around you. Adjusting your behaviour in this setting is exactly the same as experimenting with new behaviours in a work context – no more or less authentic.

Although thinking about change to re-wire the brain can help, London Business School professor Herminia Ibarra emphasises Carol Dweck's point in *Act Like a Leader, Think Like a Leader* when she says that introducing new behaviours isn't just about theoretical learning, it ultimately needs to be followed by action (she calls this the 'outside-in' experience in contrast to the 'inside-out' of focusing on theory or reflection alone).[8] It can have substantial benefits to try out something new in a safe environment, and you can share your experimentation process with colleagues around you that you trust, if that feels right.

While we might feel like there is, in truth there's no such thing as being fully natural at something; all behaviours were always new at some point or other, and all new behaviours take practice. We might just not remember the newness of those behaviours that we now feel are part of our default, but this just emphasises how much we are able to learn and adapt.[9] As we've noted throughout this book, however, some behaviours do come more naturally to some than others. British rower Helen Glover, who represented Great Britain in the 2012 and 2016 Olympics, started rowing in 2008 in her 30s, coming to the sport late compared to some of her peers who had been rowing since they were children. And yet, her natural ability enabled her to excel at the sport much quicker than someone without the same genetic makeup, and she operated at an Olympic athlete level after only training for four years. Clearly we can't all be Olympic rowers, but even if a skill such as reflection comes more easily to an introvert, we can all practice some of the quiet skills that make us better leaders, even if it's a small improvement that elevates us just a tiny bit. These marginal gains (as they're referred to by Matthew Syed[10]) can add up to a big difference over time.

You'll recall that in the previous chapter I talked about normative influence where, as humans, we're affected by the behaviours that are normalised by those around us because we're social animals who want to fit in to the group and find a community. In this sense, the more a behaviour is tried out and used – not just by introverts but also by extroverts – the higher the levels of normative influence that particular behaviour will have. So if you and others are testing out quiet leadership skills, it's culturally positive for the organisation and perpetuates itself over time; behaviour reinforces behaviour, both at the individual level through rewiring of those neurons, as well as at the group level through us influencing and being influenced by others.[11]

## Your best self

This learning and growth process – what Carol Dweck famously called the 'growth mindset'[12] – also has the benefit that we feel we always have something new to learn. Research tells us that this means that we don't ever become too bored in our day-to-day work – it helps us stay in that sweet spot between what's been called 'confused novice and bored master', which helps us be better at our jobs, and helps us approach a problem without preconceptions, which leads to more creative and better solutions.[13] For our organisations, it improves staff retention as it means we all feel stretched and challenged but without straying too far from who we really are. This is key, since taking on too many new behaviours and adopting behaviours that are too far from our starting point adds stress and needs to be done incrementally.[14] Improving our own skills also has the benefit that it improves the likelihood that we'll be more able to appreciate the skills that others bring to the table, especially if those skills are easy to master for our colleagues but we have to work harder at them ourselves. We tend to take for granted those skills that come to us naturally, but if we actively work on new skills, we'll appreciate them when we see them in others.[15] This can also help us stay curious about others, which again reduces judgement and enables us to meet our colleagues as they are and appreciate them for the skills they bring.[16]

## Too much of a good thing?

Of course, each set of strengths can be considered a weakness if overused, if used in the wrong way or at an inappropriate moment, or if used in the wrong context – that's why it's so important that we all take the time to learn more about the benefits and drawbacks of each skill, to understand how best to leverage the positives without tipping over into the negative, and also to be mindful of how the application of the skill is being perceived by those around us. Remember, we're looking to use the platinum rule, not the golden rule (do unto others as *they* prefer, not as *you* prefer). Imagine a scenario where an introvert is in charge of a project and an urgent decision needs to be made to cease work for safety reasons. In a context where people's lives are at stake, deliberating for too long and taking too much input can have a detrimental impact and lead to fatal outcomes. Here, the introvert's reflective nature needs to be overridden and the quiet leader has to take immediate and decisive action – which they are more than capable of, despite stereotype. Similarly, an extrovert in charge of the same project with the same safety pressures needs to take care not to run head first too quickly into a set of actions that could lead to equally negative outcomes – it's no use taking action if it's the wrong action. A balance between the two is usually best, and we can only find that balance if we acknowledge the value that the quiet leader brings and become more critical of the louder voices. This will help us all have a suite of behaviours at the ready that we can choose from depending on what fits the situation best, regardless of what label we might attach to that behaviour.[17]

Reflection on style and leadership effectiveness is therefore needed for both introverts and extroverts. We should all assess not just what behaviours we're choosing for each scenario we're in, but also how we might be perceived by those around us. Think of someone who enjoys meeting new people, and who might endeavour at a work party to talk to as many new people as possible. If this person interacts with someone who prefers to get to know a small number of people more in-depth, they might be seen as superficial, perhaps even boring, if they only engage in shallow small talk. Here, the extrovert's preference for meeting lots of people is no longer a strength, but will be held against them. Similarly, an introvert might hold back and let the extrovert speak in order to not be seen as rude – but the extrovert never realises that this is what's going on and believes the introvert doesn't have anything to say, not realising that this is the introvert's way of showing respect.[18] Ironically, this means the interaction comes full circle and the introvert ends up living up to the quiet stereotype as a result of the extrovert's need to talk! We know what tends to happen in organisations when the introvert and extrovert preference meets; the introvert's approach takes a back seat. As you now know, we find it less easy to see the extrovert weakness and therefore rarely ask the extrovert to change – in our examples above, the introvert would be expected to accept the superficial dialogue. However, we all benefit more if we:

- Acknowledge our own biases and heuristics, including an under-valuation of the quiet leader's skills and a tendency to overvalue the extrovert's contributions.

- Are willing to expand our skillset by practising from the buffet of skills promoted by the quiet leader, making those of increasing value in our organisations over time, because continuous usage and promotion of these skills leads to a shift in how they're recognised.

- Stay curious about the impact we have on those around us and attempt to reduce the assumptions we hold, including the assumption that others see the world the same way as us (and that our way is always the better way).

In order to do all of this, which takes work, you have to want to change and grow – but rest assured that as long as you take action and start, it will get easier, and your confidence will grow with practice. Your sense of how natural the new behaviour feels to you will also grow alongside your competence.

# A section for self-reflection

- - - - - - - - - - - - - - - - - - - - - - - - - - - - - - - - - - - - - -

- Has your preference changed over time for how you want to behave and have others behave towards you? What's driven this?
- Are the choices you make each day ones you make consciously, or are they based on habit?
- To what extent do you feel able to adjust your style depending on the needs of the situation? What, if anything, is holding you back?

- - - - - - - - - - - - - - - - - - - - - - - - - - - - - - - - - - - - - -

# part 2

—

# The quiet leader's skills

# Which areas should you focus on?

Having covered in Part 1 the problems we face as quiet leaders in business today, including our biases and how much we're all losing out by not adequately valuing the strengths of the quiet leader, Part 2 will home in on a selection of seven of the quiet leader's key skills.[1] There are two reasons for this: Firstly, to reinforce why quiet individuals are great leaders – it could be that you're a quiet individual already and just need to be reminded of the talents you naturally possess; or you might not see yourself as particularly quiet, but have a natural curiosity for learning and want to become a better leader in the mould of the quiet. Secondly, to provide very specific and tangible ways in which quiet leaders benefit an organisation. Most organisations aren't reaching their full potential because the people who have these skills as strengths aren't recognised for the value they add, meaning the skills themselves aren't fully leveraged either. I've included pointers on how you can go about adding these skills to your own leadership practice, in the hope that the following chapters will encourage you to leverage them more often. You'll recall from Part 1 that our skills and abilities aren't set in stone, but rather they can and should evolve over time, adjusting depending on what kind of leaders we want to be. If enough people use the quiet skills to a greater extent and consciously choose these attributes from the buffet of available leadership behaviours, corporate culture can change one interaction at a time and we'd all reap the benefits from a shift towards greater inclusion of a wider range of leaders – our teams will shine from being able to be themselves, our organisations will thrive and we'll all be better off. As Spencer Johnson said in the management book *Who Moved My Cheese?* doing what we've always done will only give us what we've always had.[2]

We're all unique and valuable to our organisations in different ways. All quiet leadership skills may therefore not be equally relevant for you – some might already come more naturally to you, and some might be too far from your core strengths to feel authentic even when you've tried flexing them over time. As a result, the chapters in Part 2 can be read individually where you dip in and out to the topics you're most interested in, or end to end to capture all aspects of the quiet leader's specific menu of skills. To guide you in exploring where to focus, I've developed an unscientific quiz to identify which chapters you may find more helpful to target. Answer as honestly as you can, scoring yourself from 1 to 5, where 1 is 'this is not me at all' and 5 is 'this is always me'.

| # | Question | Your score |
|---|----------|------------|
| 1 | I make sure I take quiet time for myself as often as I need | |
| 2 | I find it easy to control my emotions | |
| 3 | I am able to put a pause between my immediate feeling and the outward response | |
| 4 | I think things through before reacting | |
| 5 | I find it interesting to hear what others' views are | |
| 6 | I try to learn from past events | |
| 7 | I believe I can learn something from everyone I meet | |
| 8 | I usually feel on an even keel | |
| 9 | I find it easy to put myself in other people's shoes | |
| 10 | When I talk with someone I aim to be in the moment without considering what I will say next | |
| 11 | I usually notice details that others haven't spotted | |
| 12 | I don't feel threatened when others challenge me | |
| 13 | I believe everyone's perspectives are valid | |
| 14 | I usually don't respond to provocation | |
| 15 | I find it interesting to learn how others see me | |
| 16 | I go out of my way to be kind | |
| 17 | I use visual cues to better help me get context to what someone is saying | |
| 18 | I like to analyse and consider a situation from multiple angles | |

➤

| # | Question | Your score |
|---|----------|------------|
| 19 | I find it easy to read between the lines | |
| 20 | I am comfortable not having all the answers | |
| 21 | I seek out feedback about myself from others | |
| 22 | I recognise nuances in facial expressions | |
| 23 | I can relate to others easily | |
| 24 | I find feedback useful | |
| 25 | I am confident that I am good enough | |
| 26 | I am aware of my own strengths and weaknesses | |
| 27 | I use what I see around me to make sense of a situation | |
| 28 | I don't interrupt when others speak | |

Total your scores and match them to the list below to see which chapters you'd find more useful to focus on. You're of course still welcome to read the remaining chapters or read Part 2 end to end for the full picture!

| Add up to the total for the following questions. . . | Strength indicated |
|------------------------------------------------------|--------------------|
| Q2, Q3, Q8, Q14 | Calmness |
| Q1, Q4, Q6, Q18 | Reflection |
| Q7, Q12, Q20, Q25 | Humility |
| Q15, Q21, Q24, Q26 | Self-awareness |
| Q5, Q10, Q19, Q28 | Listening |
| Q11, Q17, Q22, Q27 | Observation |
| Q9, Q13, Q16, Q23 | Empathy |

Using the scores and the categorisation in the table above, find a total for each sub-category of quiet skills. For each skill read below to interpret how it applies to you.

| Scoring range for each strength category | Results interpretation |
|---|---|
| 17–20 | **Strong**<br><br>Your application of this skill is pervasive and consistent, and it can be considered one of your strengths. Practicing it will be useful, but it's not an area where you need to focus your efforts most. |
| 13–16 | **Sometimes strong**<br><br>Your application of this skill is generally good, but not always consistent. Practicing the skill will ensure you apply it more often. |
| 9–12 | **Sometimes weak**<br><br>Your application of this skill is inconsistent and would benefit from practice. |
| 8 or below | **Weak**<br><br>You rarely apply this skill and would benefit from practice. |

Now that you have a better understanding of which areas of quiet leadership already come more naturally to you and which ones you might need to work on, let's dive in and focus on each quiet strength in turn.

# chapter 6

---

# I think, therefore I am (*reflection*)

Reflection: The ability to stand still, take stock and consider a situation either before or after an event, and to understand how or if the lessons from the past can be leveraged in future similar scenarios. Reflection is a key part of the skillset for the quiet leader; introverts are thoughtful by nature, and with this comes an ability to focus deeply on topics, analysing a scenario from multiple angles and reflect on the pros and cons of available actions. This means slowing down decision-making prior to jumping in and ultimately allowing yourself to trust your own judgement. Reflection is also a core component of other skills such as self-awareness (which can't be effectively done without reflecting on the self) and being humble and open to challenge (which can't be done without considering that you might not have all the answers). Reflection is also key to showing empathy, which includes consideration of the perspectives that others might take. Reflection is therefore a core skill of being a quiet leader (it also came second after Observation in my online survey of key introvert skills), and because of this we'll start Part 2 by exploring the idea and practice of it. Before we dive in, let's use our existing reflection muscles to consider what benefits reflection might have.

## Exercise

In which ways do you think reflection might benefit you and the organisation you work for, as part of your leadership practice? Make a list of your suggestions.

The box below shows the core benefits I'll cover in this chapter. Perhaps you've identified additional benefits to what's included below?

## Why reflection is useful for us and our organisations

- Letting the mind wander encourages creativity and generates better ideas.
- It helps you identify what your own opinion is without interference from others, leading to more ethical decision-making.
- It encourages you to process events and associated emotions.
- It helps process new information.
- It allows for deep thinking and focus, enabling you to tackle more complex problems.
- It slows down your thinking so that the frontal cortex takes over from the amygdala, leading to decisions freer from assumptions and bias.
- It supports other leadership skills such as increased self-awareness and humility and can also improve empathy.

# Don't just do something, stand there

Most of us would like to be thought of as being reflective. It has a nice ring to it, it implies that you consider your options and don't act rashly, and it sounds a lot better than being impulsive. Like the famous *Alice in Wonderland* quote in the header, reflection requires the ability to **not** take action immediately.[1] Think not just of Alice, but also Albert Einstein's famous line that if he had an hour to solve a problem he'd spend 55 minutes thinking about it first.[2] These both represent the value we hold for reflective decision-making. The world, however, values action and speed. You'd be forgiven for thinking that a leader who delays action is indecisive and weak, but by making a conscious decision to pause you allow yourself to slow down your decision-making, not avoid it altogether. Intentionally slowing down therefore requires confidence, including the confidence to push back against artificial deadlines created for us, or which we impose on ourselves, and to feel entitled within ourselves to take the time to slow down instead of being carried away by outside forces.[3] So long as you do it with clear and conscious intent, slowing down is in itself an action.

---

## Exercise

How do you think introverts and extroverts differ in their approach to reflection?

---

We know from Chapter 2 that slowing down decision-making improves the quality of the decisions you make by allowing your frontal cortex and the intellect to take over from the emotional responses of the amygdala. Reflection aids this process; it helps you go in the right direction, not just in any direction, and reduces the assumptions and bias we make decisions with. This is often easier for introverts, who tend to think before speaking as our default position, as illustrated in Figure 6.1.

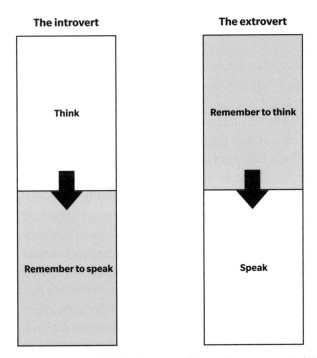

**Figure 6.1** Introverts think before speaking – for extroverts it's the other way around

In *The Slow Fix*, Carl Honoré identifies a further benefit of reflection: It enables us to pay more attention to the details and helps us analyse a situation by allowing us the space to compare our overall objective with the action we're about to take, and to consider all information at our disposal. If the action doesn't meet our objective it isn't the right action, and doing something (anything!) would mean we're in fire-fighting mode, which doesn't help us in the long run.[4] In the words of David L. Marquet, former submarine commander and author of *Turn The Ship Around!*, the vast majority of decisions – even on a weapons-grade submarine – don't need an immediate response, so we can afford to take the time needed to override our auto-pilot.[5]

# Make up your own mind

When we take the time to reflect, it helps us identify what our own position is, and once we have this it's much easier to resist persuasion from others. As a result, this form of conscious reflection helps us develop our own opinions, makes us less impressionable and leads to more ethical decision-making where we haven't been unduly influenced.[6] It helps us differentiate between what we truly know about a situation and what we assume. What can we learn from the past and which aspects don't serve a useful purpose? Is this really exactly the same scenario as last time, or are there differences that mean the response should be different? What's the real root cause of the problem we're facing, so we avoid fixing only symptoms? Consider the American military in World War II: They wanted to understand which parts of their fighter jets were most vulnerable and analysed the planes that returned with bullet damage from behind enemy lines. They found that the areas nearest to the wings, tail and centre of the plane were hit most frequently. They were about to reinforce these most-hit areas when they instead reflected and realised, with help from a research unit from Columbia University, that the really vulnerable areas were on the planes that **didn't** return.[7] They were looking at planes that were damaged but not so damaged that they couldn't turn around, with bullet holes in areas that, while hit, still allowed the plane to fly. If they had repaired these areas, they would have been strengthening areas of the plane that were already sufficiently robust. Taking the time to understand how their situation aligned with what they tried to achieve helped them avoid an investment where it wouldn't make a difference.

# Focusing the mind

It's well known that humans aren't good at multitasking. In reality there's no such thing: We're simply changing rapidly between different tasks and not truly doing more than one thing at a time.[8] Each time we attention-switch between topics it takes us time to get back into the deep focus we were in before, and deep work is therefore rarely possible without concentration on a single subject. Focus enables the brain to engage with the topic in a deeper way than if we were working on multiple things at the same time. This also helps reduce the risk of auditory and sensory overload.[9] Reflection is just another way of being introspective, and goes hand in hand with deep thinking and focusing on a single topic, which means that more complex problems can be solved. Reflective work is therefore not just better for decision-making, it also helps preserve our energy and solve tasks more efficiently.

## Get the creative juices flowing

So far I've talked about how spending time alone in reflective mode improves decision-making, but it's also good for creativity because it creates the space needed for thoughts to bubble to the surface from the sub-conscious.[10] Letting your mind wander often leads to increased idea generation and means you let your mind find inspiration within itself, generating different solutions you may not have thought of consciously, connecting dots and generating insights that we weren't able to access before.[11] How many of us have had something on the tip of our tongue and can only recall what we want to say when we stop trying to remember what it was? This is our sub-conscious helping us with the ideas, words or solution to a problem under the surface and ready for us to grab. Bill Gates recognised the value of this early, and during his tenure as CEO of Microsoft took a week off in a cottage by himself every year for a 'think week' to reflect and generate new ideas for his business (he came up with Internet Explorer on one of these trips).[12]

## Easier said than done

All of the above are material benefits of reflection, but they can be difficult to achieve. This is in part because reflection requires silence and solitude to restore our nervous system and take us off auto-pilot.[13] This can be difficult psychologically since silence and solitude are normally equated with punishment.[14] We're social beings and require connection – as a species we've survived by staying in groups and depending on each other – and historically, individuals would be banished to time alone if they'd done something the group didn't like.[15] We still do this today – think solitary confinement in prisons or a toddler on the time-out step. For this reason, many of us have a conflicted relationship with the silence and solitude that reflection requires, and it doesn't come naturally to everyone. It's also often pathologised as something that needs to be fixed – nobody has ever been called a 'loner' as a compliment. Unfortunately, when we view solitude as a problem we lose our ability to see it as something that can lead to improved leadership effectiveness.

It helps if we distinguish between the type of solitude created consciously for a particular purpose, such as decision-making and idea generation, and the type stemming from loneliness (the unwanted emotional or physical distance from others). Both generally involve spending time alone, but one is desired and necessary, and the other is not.[16] When you consider that 29 per cent of our waking time is spent alone, it's important that we're clear on the quality of that alone time and how we use it.[17] In the world's largest study on rest, results showed that quiet reflection time was particularly enthusiastically welcomed by introverts such as Gates, but it scored highly on providing benefits for both introverts as well as extroverts.[18] Extroverts, however, might need a bit more help with achieving good-quality reflective activity. So let's move on to consider what this might look like.

## Don't let yourself get distracted

In everyday life distractions are everywhere, making reflection harder.[19] Our own minds also seem to jump from topic to topic at random. So what can we do to reduce these distractions? I recommend putting your smartphone physically away from you, as a simple first step. This can mean that if you're going for a walk, you leave your phone at home. If you take yourself away from an environment with technology such as TVs, tablets, laptops or computers, it helps your ability to focus. At minimum I recommend switching off notifications on your phone, though ideally you'd be without devices altogether.

## Exercise

In which ways are you often distracted? Write down the main sources of distractions around you and consider strategies for how you can eliminate/reduce them.

| Distraction | Strategy to eliminate/reduce |
|---|---|
|  |  |
|  |  |
|  |  |
|  |  |
|  |  |

Secondly, create a structure that helps you achieve what you want rather than rely on willpower – set an alarm so you remember to make time for those walks, or hire a babysitter for a regular slot so you set aside the time you need for yourself. We often think that our future self is smarter than it is, but as we saw in Chapter 2 the human brain doesn't always know what's in our own best interest. Therefore, the more you can help your future self, the better. If you introduce these kinds of processes that help you do the right thing in future, it makes it more likely to happen, whether that's journalling, going for a walk, painting, writing, yoga, or any other activity that helps you prioritise the quiet time you need to create the space to reflect. I don't recommend reading as there are too many inputs to digest your own thoughts, but find the activity that gives you space and that works for you, so you're enjoying the process and not tempted by something more 'fun' or something that gives you an easy sense of accomplishment. Be mindful of situations more likely to take you away from your intention; for example, if you find it difficult to say 'no' to someone who asks for your help at the last minute, have a standard phrase to hand that works for the scenario such as 'I will be happy to help in an hour'.

Finally, I recommend meditation as a way to practice your reflection muscles.[20] Meditation, in particular focused meditation, helps the mind stay on a single topic without letting itself be distracted and over time builds your ability to deep-dive on a single question enabling you to focus for longer. Being focused is really about being in the here and now, and focused meditation is therefore useful if you're using reflection for problem-solving and analysis (if you're using it for creativity and idea generation, you want to let the mind wander, but paying attention to the mind and where it strays is useful for both purposes, and helps build the reflection muscle over time).

Once you've got the routine, you prioritise the time to reflect and you've built your mind muscles to do so effectively, your reflective time should feel rejuvenating and refreshing, as well as productive.

## Safety in numbers

So far I've focused on reflection as a solitary activity, because reflection is a one-person job; however, it doesn't necessarily follow that it has to be done on your own. You need to determine for yourself the best environment for you – and reflection may be a communal affair for some, where you do your best thinking around other people. Many introverts (like me) prefer to work from coffee shops or libraries; they're communal spaces where you get a fill of social connection but still allow for solitude. I wrote parts of this book in coffee shops around East London because I'm better able to focus with background sounds. That's not to say reflection is a group activity, but for some people like myself, reflection and deep thinking work best when surrounded by others without having to interact. Being with others creates a sense of forced focus where you have a purpose for yourself but you're not on your own. The key is that you identify the right environment for you, whether that's completely on your own in a forest or in a communal setting where others are also doing their own thing, together.

In the context of groups, let's also briefly discuss ways in which you as a leader can encourage reflection in your teams. Humans don't think effectively in groups – we talk, exchange ideas, we compromise and we challenge each other; interpersonal communication serves all sorts of important purposes, but thinking isn't one of them.[21] This is compounded by extroversion: Just because someone talks doesn't mean those thoughts are fully formed or well considered. We already know that slowing down decision-making is beneficial for the quality of those decisions, and this is also true within groups: The more you can facilitate a slowing down of the conversations that lead to decisions or recommendations, the better the end result will be.[22] You can do this, for instance, by making sure that everyone in the group gets a chance to speak, checking that no single person dominates the discussion or is louder than others, by monitoring the extent to which individuals are being interrupted, by allowing silence and by creating an expectation that reflective behaviour is what you're looking for – on your watch nobody will be rewarded when they talk just for the sake of talking. Ahead of each group session, allow time for preparation, provide a clear agenda and outline the purpose for the meeting and what you need from participants. Some may also find that it helps to include some prep time in the meeting itself (just like that Amazon example I mentioned in Chapter 4), and to encourage critique and challenge. I also find that it helps the culture of the team if you emphasise that you want to hear all ideas, not just 'good' ideas, to reduce the likelihood of self-censure for those who tend to do this. This kind of setting then places emphasis on the importance of the words we use and encourages your team to bring nuance to the discussion when they talk.[23] When everyone in the group is more comfortable with what their own personal position is, it also has the benefit that it reduces the risk of group-think.

## Too much of a good thing

As much as we all want to be reflective and thoughtful individuals, we also need to take care not to overdo it. I mentioned earlier that all strengths can become weaknesses if they're used too much or not used with due care, and so too with the ability to reflect deeply. Reflection by its very nature requires introspection, and if we over-use this skill it can lead to rumination, the practice of going over and over something in our minds in a repeated pattern without a clear outcome, which can contribute to anxiety and even lead to depression.[24] Therefore, take particular care of how you use the reflective time and set defined start and end times for the activity, with a clear goal for your session, to reduce the risk of that rumination and self-doubt taking over and it becoming a negative habit.

While reflection is an action in its own right, we don't want to leave it at that – we need follow-through from the thinking we're doing. We can consider this when we set our intention at the beginning – what's the outcome we're looking for? Is it a list of pros and cons, a decision, a conclusion about what our view is after weighing up evidence for and against, or something else that's tangible and specific? Whatever the outcome we want, reflection is rarely the end state, and we should make sure there's a clear next step for us to take afterwards.

Until we have a strong enough reflective muscle, or if the topic at hand is not one we actively want to engage with (but we know we should), the final risk to highlight is that we might create distractions to replace the reflective work.[25] Some call this 'busy work', where we feel like we're being productive and training our reflective muscles, but actually we're only tackling small topics or letting our minds wander when we're trying to problem-solve. To avoid this, it's important that we notice what our minds are doing, and learn from each experience so we understand better what works for us and what doesn't. When practising how best to integrate reflective behaviours into your own repertoire, the following table can be a useful reference point:

| Do | Don't |
|---|---|
| Take time for yourself and look for opportunities to practice | Expect results immediately |
| Set a clear and conscious intent for each session, such as a particular problem or a goal you'd like to achieve (e.g. generate ideas for a new business) | Focus on more than one thing at a time |
| Introduce processes that create structure to prioritise reflection, such as hiring a babysitter for a fixed time every week or setting an alarm to remind you of your intention to pause | Encourage or create distractions |
| Have a standard phrase to hand if you find it difficult to avoid interruptions, e.g. 'Thanks for the heads up. I'll be happy to talk in an hour' | Visit areas/venues where you're more likely to be interrupted |
| Form the idea before talking | Talk before the thought is processed |
| Practise when you're relaxed and not in fight, flight or freeze mode – this effort works best when you're doing it preventively | Give in to the temptation to engage in 'busy work', which makes you feel like you're making progress, but doesn't exercise your reflective muscles |
| Make a habit of questioning yourself – your views are based on your background, assumptions and biases, and may not be the only truth out there | Apply past knowledge to the current situation without assessing its validity – treat each scenario as unique |

| | |
|---|---|
| If you want to be creative, let your mind wander – this helps ideas bubble to the surface | Generate so many ideas that you're left with 'analysis paralysis' |
| Ensure you make conscious decisions after reflecting | Stop the reflective work at the point of idea generation – action needs to follow |
| Figure out what works best for you – it can include journalling, a walk in the forest, meditation, a solo lunch, yoga, or anything else that gives you space (including communally such as working from coffee shops or libraries) | Take inspiration without assessing it for yourself – a practice that works for others might not work for you |
| Assess what's working and what isn't | Assume that your skill will improve automatically |

# A section for self-reflection

- How can you add reflection to your own daily habits? What have you tried already? When was the last time you took the time to be quiet and alone?

- What can you do to encourage your team to incorporate reflection in their daily routine to make this practice easier for them?

- What works/doesn't work about your current approach to reflection? What evidence exists that the steps you're taking are the best ones for you?

- How good are you at noticing when your mind is drifting aimlessly?

- In which situations do you tend to revert to fire-fighting and taking action before thinking? What can you do to turn this around?

# chapter 7

---

# Human, know thyself
## (self-awareness)

One of the themes of this book is that, in order to be a good leader, you need to consciously select the behaviours you want to get the outcome you're looking for. To actively select your behaviours, however, you need to be aware of what's going on inside yourself first, as not doing so means you'll always be at the mercy of reacting to whatever life and other people throw your way without taking control of your own responses. I'll therefore spend this chapter discussing self-awareness, what it is and the steps you can take to acquire more of it.

## What does it mean to be self-aware?

Self-awareness is the ability to see ourselves clearly, warts and all. By its nature, the 'self' is the individual, the focus of 'me' and 'myself', and has an inward, introspective emphasis on thoughts, feelings and sensations. It's being aware that you're aware – as humans we're the only species on earth with this ability.[1] This doesn't just mean having an understanding of who we are and our values – it also means seeing our own behaviours and uncovering some of the deeper motivations underneath, to understand what drives us. When we think we make a conscious decision or behave a certain way, part of that decision-making process also involves an unconscious layer. I mentioned in Chapter 2 that the amygdala provides us with a very primal, emotional response that can only be overridden if we slow down our thinking to activate the more rational part of our brains. Those mechanisms don't just affect how we see others; they also affect how and how clearly we see ourselves. What's tricky is that often, as much as we try to uncover our own motivations, some of our inner workings remain hidden and we need to work hard to access them – and indeed some parts might never be truly known.[2]

Introverts have a head start in this work because all self-awareness starts with introspection and, as we know, introverts are generally more introspective. This doesn't mean that introverts are automatically better leaders any more than extroverts are better because of our inherent traits, but we can use this head start to be the best version of ourselves – if we need time between meetings to recharge, we can make that happen; if we prefer to prepare in advance to anticipate potential objections to our arguments, that's a useful insight too. Crucially, self-awareness also means having an understanding of how others see us.[3] In a society of finger-pointing and polarisation, introverts also have a benefit here because we're generally less attached to any specific outcome or idea, enabling us more objectively to see our own role in a particular situation and incorporating the views of others.[4]

# Ignorance is bliss

Most of us think we're self-aware, but in reality, truly knowing yourself and your motivations is a tricky thing to achieve. In Chapter 2

I mentioned the Dunning–Krueger effect where the least competent are often the most confident. So too with self-awareness – those who think they're self-aware often have the largest blind spots. Societal pressures don't help: We live in a society of blame where it's hard to reflect on our own behaviours and our own role in an outcome without being made a scapegoat for anything that didn't quite go to plan; there's a reason injury lawyers advise their clients to never admit fault on the scene of a crime! In society today, there's a big emphasis on leaders projecting an image of self-assuredness and certainty, and this reduces the likelihood that individuals delve more deeply into their own motivations and behaviours. And no wonder we hesitate to look inward; we all have weaknesses that we might be scared to explore lest we find out that we're not such nice people after all. That co-worker who joined after you and got promoted before you? Maybe your dislike of them isn't because of their poor sales pitch in the last presentation to the board. Maybe it's actually jealousy. Being genuinely self-aware requires having difficult conversations with yourself; it means finding out truths about your own motivations that might not be so pleasant and it might involve hearing from others their observations and perceptions that you find surprising and even hurtful.

Both the internal and the external lenses are key for self-awareness – it's not possible to be fully self-aware with input only from yourself about what you're really like – and both can be equally difficult to achieve. But the benefits are worth it – and you might even uncover some strengths in the process. The quadrant in Figure 7.1 shows the different sources of information about ourselves where we might not have the full picture, and nor do others, called the Johari Window.[5] Because we and others individually don't have the complete picture, combining the two for a more holistic self-awareness picture is crucial.

True self-awareness means opening up as many of these quadrants as possible, and the closer we get to merging the picture we have of ourselves with the ones that others have of us, the more authentic we can be.

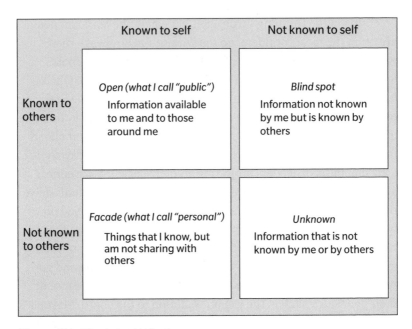

**Figure 7.1** The Johari Window

# Exercise

Create a list of adjectives (positive and negative, such as kind, impatient, generous, etc.). Then, map them along the 'known to self' *vertical* of the Johari Window if they apply to you. Leave aside the adjectives that don't apply. Ask someone you trust to select from the same list (even the ones you have mapped already) and let them select the words they feel describe you (along the *horizontal*). Those words selected by others <u>but not by you</u> belong in the Blind Spot quadrant and give you new insight into how you're perceived. This can be used as a starting point for further conversation. A section later in this chapter will help you identify your trusted advisors if you don't already have a list to hand.

# The benefits to your business

Self-awareness has a bit of a bad rep in the business world – it's too 'out there', and comes with too much self-disclosure and risk of being too vulnerable around people who, in the wrong corporate cultures, will leverage what they find out to stab you in the back. In a world where leaders are expected to show certainty and have the courage of their convictions, self-awareness can be seen as dangerous because it might lead to behavioural experimentation, and it increases transparency about our own struggles and things we're not sure about – all of which is scary stuff and might in turn lead to some leaders not embracing self-awareness for what it can give them. This is a shame, because research shows that self-awareness is the single best predictor of leadership success.[6] It's also good for the bottom line – a study by executive search firm Korn Ferry of 7000 employees across 486 companies showed that organisations with poorer financial performance had leaders with 20 per cent higher levels of blind spots (where I think I'm good at something and you think I'm not), and 79 per cent were more likely to have low self-awareness. Low self-awareness creates cultures where improvement opportunities are seen as a threat, and where feedback is infrequent and of poor quality, whereas higher self-awareness in leaders gives those organisations the ability to focus on employee strengths and compensate for weaknesses, while also enabling those leaders to be more objective and focus on what's best for the organisation rather than focusing on their own ego.[7]

# Know thyself

Let's start with the internal view first: By exploring your own motivations and becoming more self-aware, you'll be tapping into a huge source of strength as it puts you in a better position to more actively choose your own behaviours. You'll also more easily be able to achieve your goals by reducing self-sabotage where your underlying motivations are hidden from you and you therefore take actions that go against your own best interests. Uncovering these hidden drivers will better align your behaviours with your conscious intent. Consider the example of Matt, a senior audit executive who year after year was being passed over for promotion, but kept getting small pay increases because he was a good individual contributor the company didn't want to lose. Matt's conscious belief was that the pay increases were sufficient because his primary driver was to provide for his wife and two young children, and the increases were large enough to support this belief. However, he also had a strong subconscious drive to be publicly recognised, and the pay increases didn't give him that. His subconscious therefore led him to express views about the inadequacy of senior management's decision-making, which they became aware of, reducing Matt's chances of a future promotion even further. Until Matt becomes aware of his deeper motivation for public recognition and how it links with his behaviour, nothing will change. When he understands how important public recognition is to him, he can leave the company for a promotion or adjust his behaviour to one more promotion-worthy in the culture he's in, but until then he'll be locked in a negative cycle of unmet needs.

Research shows that when we know ourselves we're happier, and when our behaviours are integrated with our underlying drivers and values we make better decisions and are more effective leaders. It's therefore worth the effort, but exploring your own motivations, feelings and views is tricky at best. To successfully uncover as much self-insight as possible, try using a structured model such as the one shown in Figure 7.2 (adapted from Scouller[8]), which takes you through the various stages of exploring what might be going on underneath the obvious first layer of your mind. It involves taking a particular concern you have, or something that isn't working as you'd like, being curious about what you find and turning the scenario around in your mind to look at it from different angles.

For Matt, going through this exercise would mean acknowledging his need for recognition and understanding how others (especially senior management) see him. Figure 7.3 shows what Matt's self-assessment might look like for his situation.[9] For Matt, his ego is

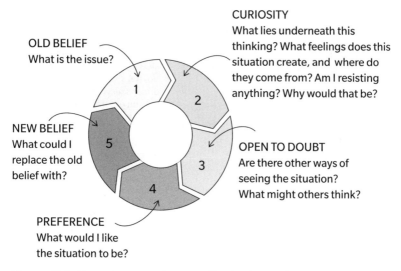

**CURIOSITY**
What lies underneath this thinking? What feelings does this situation create, and where do they come from? Am I resisting anything? Why would that be?

**OLD BELIEF**
What is the issue?

**NEW BELIEF**
What could I replace the old belief with?

**OPEN TO DOUBT**
Are there other ways of seeing the situation? What might others think?

**PREFERENCE**
What would I like the situation to be?

**Figure 7.2** Questions to ask yourself to look at a situation from several angles

a blocker: For others it might be fear, shame, pride or just simple inertia.

Unfortunately, the more senior you are the less likely you are to be self-aware.[10] This is partly because people stop telling you what you need to hear out of self-preservation and self-interest if they don't think you'll take the input well, and partly because many of us, when we climb the career ladder, think we don't need to change (it's worked so far, right?) and therefore become less willing to learn and adapt. To be able to manage others well, however, you first have to be able to manage yourself, and the best way to do that is to keep learning, and updating your skills and knowledge.[11]

I mentioned initially that those who find it easier to be introspective, such as introverts, have a head start in the self-awareness game; however, reflection and introspection aren't the only required ingredients. There's no direct correlation between reflective activity on its own and increased self-awareness. A study by psychology professor Constantine Sedikides shows this clearly: A number of prisoners were asked to self-assess along a range of categories, including how law-abiding they were compared to those on the outside, and remarkably

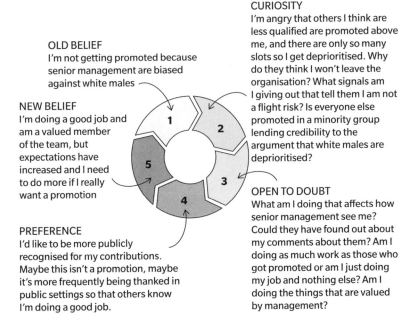

**OLD BELIEF**
I'm not getting promoted because senior management are biased against white males

**CURIOSITY**
I'm angry that others I think are less qualified are promoted above me, and there are only so many slots so I get deprioritised. Why do they think I won't leave the organisation? What signals am I giving out that tell them I am not a flight risk? Is everyone else promoted in a minority group lending credibility to the argument that white males are deprioritised?

**NEW BELIEF**
I'm doing a good job and am a valued member of the team, but expectations have increased and I need to do more if I really want a promotion

**OPEN TO DOUBT**
What am I doing that affects how senior management see me? Could they have found out about my comments about them? Am I doing as much work as those who got promoted or am I just doing my job and nothing else? Am I doing the things that are valued by management?

**PREFERENCE**
I'd like to be more publicly recognised for my contributions. Maybe this isn't a promotion, maybe it's more frequently being thanked in public settings so that others know I'm doing a good job.

**Figure 7.3** Questions that Matt could have asked himself to generate greater self-insight

the inmates considered themselves more law-abiding than those not in prison! Objectively, this seems hard to fathom, but it exemplifies the extent to which we don't see ourselves very clearly.[12]

Given that self-awareness is so elusive, to turn introspection into insight about ourselves, your likelihood of success will increase if you don't look for a single underlying reason for your behaviour – we're complex beings and there's rarely only one explanation for why we behave the way we do. It's more helpful and practical to look at what's going on (what are you feeling, what's another way to see the situation, what needs to change) rather than the **why** of it. A famous study by researchers Dutton and Aron tested this out in practice by putting a beautiful woman at the end of a long suspension bridge just outside Vancouver in Canada – she asked adult males crossing the bridge research questions and offered to follow up afterwards by giving out her phone number. They also did a control set on a sturdier bridge nearby. The men on the suspension bridge, a wobbly bridge that induced fear and generated an increased heart rate, called her back in a higher proportion than those on the sturdy bridge. When asked why, those on the suspension bridge attributed their action to her looks rather than their increased heart rate from being on the more dangerous bridge. The woman hadn't changed, but the men on the wobbly bridge thought their increased heart rate must have meant she was attractive, and therefore asked her out: As humans we find the easiest, most plausible reason to explain our behaviours, but those reasons aren't always the true ones and not always accurate.[13]

## Example

Think of a situation you're unhappy about and identify the belief that sits underneath the unhappiness. What do you uncover?

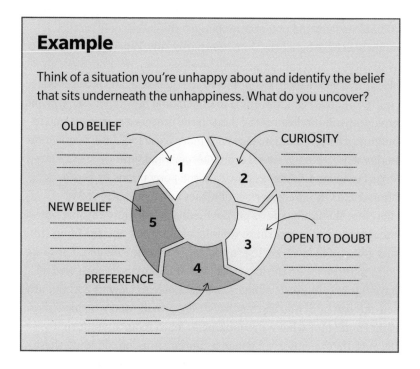

## The perceptions of others

Others often see us more clearly than we see ourselves, and the views of those around us are therefore extremely useful sources for enhanced self-awareness; think about how many times you've observed a romantic relationship from afar and just known that it won't work out long term. Seeing more clearly how you come across to others puts you in a better position to adjust behaviours based on a fuller set of information, should you choose to do so. It means that you can more easily see the same version of you as those who, say, make hiring and promotion decisions, which enables you to adjust your approach or more easily learn from setbacks. Matt, the executive who never got the promotion he wanted, never sought feedback from others and even said he was 'too old to change'. I don't know why Matt never asked for input from those around him who wanted him to succeed, but a fear of what he might hear could have been part of it. Not only would an honest conversation with a trusted colleague have provided valuable insight and potentially changed the course of his career, it might also have benefitted him interpersonally. When you have more awareness of how colleagues at all levels see you, relationships can blossom as you're more easily able to see their side, and it helps reduce conflict. If done right, the effort to understand how others see you and providing self-disclosures to others in the process can in itself lead to building stronger relationships with more trust and closer connection. In this sense, self-awareness is an interpersonal skill.

As I noted in Chapter 2, however, the perceptions from others often come with their own set of biases and assumptions. We therefore shouldn't take as gospel feedback from just anyone, but we should carefully select those we take views from, and the input from this group of helpful, caring supporters can be invaluable. Those we want to listen to are those people that – close to us or not – we feel have our best interests at heart, who are able to view us without any self-interest built into the feedback they provide and who have the right context for what we're looking to learn more about (usually because they've observed you in a similar situation). Finding these unicorn feedback-givers isn't easy, but when you do, their input can be a huge source of useful knowledge about how you come across, and they can give you a healthy challenge and nuggets of wisdom. Once you've determined who they are, you need to let yourself be vulnerable with them and explain what you're trying to achieve, the context and what area you're looking for input on. Be specific in your questions and introduce the reason why you're asking (e.g. if you feel that your behaviour might be holding you back at work, or

that you don't understand why a particular interaction went awry).
Also explain why you're asking *them* specifically. Your list of trusted
advisors might change from scenario to scenario.[14] Once you have
their input, make sure to look for patterns as these are the nuggets
that help give insight. Feedback on your behaviour in a specific
situation can also be useful, but may not be pervasive and therefore
less representative as a path to building self-awareness, so it's the
patterns you're looking for.

## Exercise

Think of an area where things aren't quite going to plan and
where you'd like to expand your self-awareness. What would
your list of trusted advisors look like? (Input from all groups
below may not be where your unicorn feedback providers sit,
but the categories give structure to identifying them.)

| Colleagues | Current/former managers | Friends | Mentors |
|---|---|---|---|
|  |  |  |  |
|  |  |  |  |
|  |  |  |  |
|  |  |  |  |

## Taking it all in

Self-awareness is a skill and therefore the acceptance that we all
need to work on it and the willingness to do so are key. You'll recall
the Dunning–Krueger effect, so be aware that the more you think
you know, the more you probably need to learn. Being open to trying
new things, and taking feedback on what works and what doesn't
from those experiments, is a key step in the self-awareness process

to avoid it becoming a purely theoretical exercise. In *The Slow Fix,* Carl Honoré points out that nobody wants firefighters or surgeons to experiment on the job, but interpersonal experiments can safely be done in most professions – after all, for most of us there are no life-or-death implications of trying out a new behaviour or two.

Hearing potentially difficult messages in the advice you receive and in what you uncover as part of expanded self-insights and through your experiments can throw up a lot of baggage and reveal our own psychological blockers. If we don't feel good about ourselves – and we all have areas where we're not always on top of the world – this will come out in our response to the various self-awareness practices we undertake, and any explorations beneath the surface. This can be a feeling of inadequacy, not being likeable, or feeling insignificant, and it will colour the way we react to what we find. Sometimes, we might feel defensive and project on to others what we feel in ourselves – say someone in your team tells you that a request you made was unclear to them. If this touches a nerve and triggers the underlying feeling that you're not a good communicator, you might become defensive and feel that your request was in fact clear but that the team member wasn't listening properly. All of this feeds an unhealthy cycle which limits your ability to learn more about yourself,[15] and it's therefore no surprise that we don't have a complete picture of ourselves – even though it might feel like we do.

For these reasons it's helpful if we have a model to follow to help us understand what's going on within ourselves when we react to what we uncover, since the areas where we have the strongest emotional responses are often the ones we need to pay attention to the most. The mindfulness model in Figure 7.4 is a useful tool to help us course-correct our own behaviour based on inputs received both through self-enquiry and based on feedback from others.[16]

The starting point can be a new observation or data point from yourself or others – it can be something major like getting fired, or as small as an offhand comment from someone that made you curious, or an event you had a particularly strong reaction to even if nobody else was around. Usually you won't be aware of this until after it's happened, but once you're aware you can then look out for

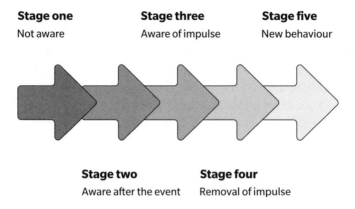

**Figure 7.4** Mindfulness model

it the next time it happens and perhaps at that point notice it *during* the response. This allows you to explore what made you have the response in the first place so that in future you can replace this with a new behaviour. It all starts with being aware of what's going on in yourself and being curious about what's happening rather than critical. This is easier if you're not under stress.[17] Once you've noticed a pattern you can start to experiment with making different choices in similar situations in future.[18] Mindfulness enables you to be in the present and notice what's going on with your body, your thoughts, your feelings and your values – it's not just about observation and not at all about removing all thought, but rather an active choice to look inward and explore what you find. This isn't always pleasant, but sitting with those feelings and exploring them non-judgementally is a key part of the exercise and helps grow your self-awareness, which can help you understand and take in more of the input you get from others and to open your mind to see yourself more objectively.

As you experiment with these stages, be patient and have compassion with yourself and remember that change doesn't happen overnight. Monitor your inner dialogue for criticism – I know it might seem like that critical voice helped you get to where you are, but research indicates that self-compassion is actually a better indicator of future performance than a critical internal monologue.[19] Studies show that when participants gave themselves self-compassionate responses, they were more likely to have a more positive mental state and accept personal responsibility rather than shifting blame on to others.[20] As we learn more about ourselves with input from self-enquiry and from others, being kind to ourselves as we improve our skills is therefore beneficial both for ourselves and our colleagues.

# A section for self-reflection

- How self-aware do you think you are? Could you be a Dunning–Krueger victim?
- Which of the exercises in this chapter did you find harder to apply? Is there anything to learn from the resistance you feel or the emotions brought to the surface relating to those topics?
- How do you intend to practice self-awareness going forward?

# chapter 8

---

# See what I mean? *(observation)*

In the previous chapter I looked inward; in this chapter I'll move outward and focus on the skill involved with looking clearly at others. Being observant means having attention to details about what's going on around you and using what you can see with your own eyes, such as observing body language and facial expressions or people's behaviour more generally, to help understand more about a situation and to interpret interactions between them and us – or between others. This insight can come from watching others interact, from a conversation we're part of ourselves, or from observing others from afar, such as seeing someone in a new and unknown environment. Sixty five per cent of what we communicate is non-verbal, so being able to spot and interpret this large chunk of what other people are communicating can be an incredibly powerful leadership skill in your arsenal.

Many mistakenly think of 'observation' as passive, something that just happens as part of doing nothing but sit back and watch – but in reality, observation done well is an activity that helps you obtain information, and it requires attention to detail, staying focused for prolonged periods, and an ability to step back and take in what's around us. These are all automatic tendencies for the introverts, making us natural observers; in my online survey of introvert skills, those surveyed listed observation as the top skill they associated with introverts.[1] I often say that one of my key strengths is my ability to switch between operational detail and higher-level strategy effortlessly, and this comes from my quiet nature. So let's look at each of these elements in turn.

## Take a look around

When we actively observe, we acquire additional information that helps us identify important context such as what others are feeling, what the mood in the room is and how messages are landing – in other words, important content not being said using words. This information is useful for you as a leader because it helps to understand if the people you work with are engaged, if they understand what you're saying or if they're unclear on anything, if they need support, and whether there are underlying disagreements to what you're communicating – all of which are crucial for delivery and execution as well as for team cohesiveness. If someone in your team doesn't agree with the direction of travel, or if they don't understand what they're being asked to do, they're not going to deliver to the best of their ability. This in turn will affect the quality of their work and the successful execution of your or the company's strategy. It's not the case in real life that once a strategy has been set, everyone jumps aboard eager to deliver – often people appear to agree to an idea in the moment, but without being fully behind it when it comes to actual delivery. It's invaluable to be able to determine where this is likely to occur. If you know where key people (including your team) see stumbling blocks or pitfalls before they're willing to buy into your idea, you're in a better position to take action to bring those people along from the beginning.

Skilled observation can also help improve individual relationships as it enables you to better understand what your colleagues and your team members need, and the communication style they prefer. This puts you in a position to create an environment where they can thrive and work with you in the best possible way. As a good leader you want to be inclusive, and help others to feel included, and this can best be done when you understand their true feelings and views.[2] This is true not just for established working relationships, but can also help you identify whether a prospective new hire is a good fit before they start. They might say they're a great team player, but if when asked to give examples their eyes dart around the room and they start to fidget, there's a disconnect between what they say and how they look. This might mean you want to explore this area further before extending an offer for the role (given the situation, it could be that they're just nervous).[3]

In a group setting, observing others helps you as a leader to manage the dynamic and emotions of the collective. If two members of your team have a disagreement, this will spill over into all interactions they have, so being able to identify this will make your team function better. Good observation has also been shown to improve team and individual performance even when there are no conflicts – a study from the Netherlands showed that people with good observation skills are more creative than others, and it doesn't matter whether those skills were inherent or acquired.[4]

Observation is also useful before making decisions or shaping your message as you go, as it enables you to pick up on cues from the group and creates the space for them to provide their own input that might shape the end result.[5] An example of this is Miriam – a financial services professional about to propose the implementation of a new set of performance metrics for her department. She was presenting to the executive committee when she noticed that the global head was busy on his phone. She could see from where she was sitting that he was on YouTube so she knew he wasn't engaged in urgent company business. His behaviour was influencing the rest of the group, and she knew that if she didn't get his attention she'd be at risk of not being taken seriously as well as missing out on the sign-off she was looking for. It was unprofessional of the global head to be on his phone, but Miriam needed to focus on bringing him back in the room. Her observation that the global head's attention was elsewhere helped her stop her presentation and ask for input from the group, which led to the executive looking up from the phone and interrupting what he was doing. Ultimately it also helped prevent the behaviour of the global head from influencing the others in the room negatively, which could over time have affected her career with the company. In this scenario, the global head chose to express his disagreement (or disinterest) by focusing his attention elsewhere, but we can also observe facial expressions to achieve the same. This is particularly true for extroverts as they usually have more expressive body language.[6] Regardless of whether those around you are introverts or extroverts, however, the act of observing helps improve the interaction and increases the likelihood that you'll get the outcome you're aiming for.

## Pay attention to details

Observation means focusing on what's outside of ourselves while at the same time internally interpreting what we observe, and this focus comes easier to the introvert who tends to sit back and take in information as a default. Our highly developed attention to detail helps when observing nuanced facial expressions or seeing the little behaviours that might not seem to matter but that actually say a great deal about someone's true feelings.[7] This is central to the work of researcher Paul Ekman, whose work is the basis of the TV show *Lie to Me* (I recommend it!) – the premise of the show and Ekman's area of research is what he refers to as 'microexpressions'. These are the minute and milliseconds worth of expressions that reveal how we really feel before our conscious mind takes over and before we show to the world what we decide to show, rather than what our immediate emotional response is.[8] In the TV series the lead detective was able to catch killers by being able to spot these microexpressions as they give away that the suspect is lying; in your day-to-day they might help you interact more productively with colleagues and team members. If you pay close attention, that split second worth of an initial reaction can, if you spot it, give you an indication of a person's true feelings and enable you to explore their opinion further.

All of this requires us to also be present in the moment and focus. If you're not present, it's much harder to both observe well and to build your observational muscle.[9] If you observe in a careful and intentional way, you're more likely to accurately interpret what you see and be able to take advantage of what you find. Several exercises can help you build this skill, including the mindfulness exercise below which helps you to focus on a single item, by staying in the moment, and in turn also practice the act of observation itself.[10]

## Exercise

Grab a small piece of fruit or something else edible, and assess it from the perspectives below. Describe it using each of these categories:

- shape
- colour
- texture
- smell

As an example, a raisin could be labelled as having an 'oval' shape, be wrinkled in texture and brown in colour. We can introduce more nuance and play around with the descriptions, making the raisin 'shaped like a UFO', or 'the colour of a dried leaf in the autumn'. Be creative and expand how you see the item and in turn other items and situations around you.

# It's the little things

In the self-awareness chapter I mentioned that the body is often the first place we notice that something is going on within ourselves – we might feel that we've clenched our fists and realise we're angry about something, or our teeth chatter if we're nervous.[11] The body is also the first place we see it when observing what's going on with others; a tense jaw might indicate that they don't like an argument you're making, folded arms might show that they have reservations, and a raised eyebrow might signal that they don't think what you're saying is realistic. If there's a disconnect between what we really think and what we say, most of us have little 'tells' – our individual ways for the truth to leak out from our bodies – giving away our true opinion even if no words are used. Like the lead detective in *Lie to Me*, or a good poker player, we can learn to spot these signs of disconnect. There's no absolute list of what to look for – it can be a tensing of the jaw, biting of lips, smiles that don't go all the way to the eyes, or something else altogether. The real key is to find differences to how the person normally behaves and their usual body language. If your partner never crosses their arms and suddenly starts to do so when you ask them where they were last night, that could be worth paying closer attention to. If they always cross their arms, perhaps it isn't. While we shouldn't assume that those around us at home or in the workplace are trying to hide anything from us, it can be useful to see this as a way to get to know those people better and have more meaningful dialogue.

Crucially, observation isn't useful just in the context of body language – if you observe others closely, you might also spot that your colleague Jane from Compliance always responds via email regardless of what medium you contact her through, that Keith spends very little time at his desk and instead hovers in the kitchen having small chats with colleagues most of the day, or that John from Accounts tends to take the long route to the bathroom. It's normally when people don't know they're being observed, and when they relax, that we can see their true nature or feelings. We can use this to make them more comfortable, feel more included and to understand if there's anything blocking the outcomes we're looking for.[12]

# Seeing is believing

All of the above scenarios, if we add some curiosity, will help us understand those individuals better. Keith might not have enough challenging tasks on, or perhaps his deadlines are at risk; Jane might like to think things through before providing her opinion; John might be on a diet and doesn't want to be tempted by the lovely smells from the canteen so he walks around it. These are all assumptions, however – and we know from Chapter 2 what that means for the accuracy of our interpretations. We don't actually know if John is on a diet or if he is actually avoiding Peter whose office is near the kitchen, or if there's some other reason entirely behind his detours. I once interviewed a future colleague and years later, once we'd worked together for a while, he shared that he thought I'd been crossing my legs because I didn't think he should be hired – in reality I had discovered a run on my tights that I wanted to cover up but was very excited to have him onboard!

Despite the risk of misunderstanding, for observation to be meaningful we do need to interpret what we see. That's the only way that noticing what's going on around us can help us make sense of the situations and people we come in contact with. However, there's a difference between interpretation to generate deeper understanding and interpretation using only our assumptions, and thinking that these are automatically correct. To interpret as accurately as possible, as well as being aware of our own biases and making a conscious effort to go beyond stereotype, we need to also engage with the relevant individuals directly.[13] As I noted in Chapter 7, the perceptions of others need to be commented on by those others, not interpreted by us alone. Discussing negative interpretations with a third party never leads to anything productive (they might just agree with you to avoid conflict), and you'll likely influence their view even if you're wrong. An experiment by psychologist Solomon Asch[14] shows how impressionable we are when faced with others' opinions. Test subjects were asked to look at an image of three straight lines and compare it to an original one. The first line was short, the second much longer and the third line clearly the same length as the first one. Sounds simple, right? Indeed, the test subjects correctly identified that line three was the same as the original line when alone. However, when they were put in a group of others (all hired actors, unbeknownst to the test subject) and told that lines one and two were the same length, the test subjects ended up agreeing with the group even though they'd previously, when on their own, stated the correct answer. This was even when the answers given by the others in the group were obviously wrong! It's easy to be influenced by others even when we have our minds made up and even when we have our own physical senses to rely on, even harder when the topic is an impression of someone. Instead of discussing with others, we should therefore always discuss with the person we want to learn to understand better, so we interpret with support of direct dialogue. This helps prevent our observations from turning into a misconstruction of reality, and ensures that what we take away improves performance and relationships instead of damaging them.

Similarly to the misunderstandings that might occur when we're the observers, we might also not be fully aware of the signals we send out to others ourselves – sometimes our actions can be misunderstood or our faces don't send the signals our minds think they're sending. I've been surprised a number of times when I see photos of myself and recall that I had intended to look sombre and instead the end result was, inexplicably, smug! The exercise below will help you start to explore this using yourself as a test subject.[15]

## Exercise

Stand in front of a mirror or record yourself on video. Try different facial expressions for different emotions – such as anger, happiness, frustration, boredom. Does your face look like you expect it to? If not, how might others misinterpret you when you're being observed by them?

# Detach yourself

Finally, the introvert's ability to step back is key to skilful observation. If any of us get too involved in what we're observing, we lose some of our capacity to take in what we see.[16] This stems in part from the fact that when we're in an interaction, most of us are generally focused on things that aren't related to the observation itself, such as the next thing we want to say, or how we come across. I've mentioned before how bad humans are at multitasking – when we're part of the interaction this reduces the bandwidth available to observe because of the cost associated with switching between the two activities (observing is an activity). There's therefore a dilution of your attention when you try to both be part of the situation as well as observing it.[17]

## Exercise

Recall a recent conversation. It doesn't matter what the topic was or whether it was a friendly chat or a tense discussion. Watch yourself from the outside and observe both of you. Explain to yourself what you see as if you weren't part of the conversation but a third party. When you imagine the scene now, do you see anything you didn't notice at the time?

An example of the impact of participation on our ability to observe is the 'gorilla and basketball' experiment.[18] You may have heard about this study before. Researchers asked participants, who watched the game on a TV screen, to count the number of times the ball was passed between the two teams. The study participants were so immersed in this task of counting passes that they didn't spot that a man in a gorilla costume walked slowly across the court halfway through the game. The game was being recorded, and it was only when the video was re-played that many of the participants noticed him. This is what happens when we get too involved with what we observe – our brains aren't able to cope and we see only one part of the picture. This means we lose the holistic view of what we're looking at unless we build our muscle for observation. Introverts have a head start, as a group that often actively chooses to take a step back to assess a scenario before deciding what to do.

## Gotta start somewhere

As you've by now no doubt realised, observation isn't always straightforward, but the beauty is that once you've started to notice something – whether that's a body signal from the person you're talking to, a pattern of behaviour, or the dynamic between your team members – you can start to make different choices that might yield better outcomes. Introverts generally pick up on these little cues quite easily, so it can be disappointing when others aren't able to do the same.[19] However, with more focus on observation as a skill that can be enhanced, more people will be able to see connections that might not have been obvious to them before. That 'aha!' moment of understanding when someone's reaction finally makes sense will improve communication immeasurably.

---

### Exercise

Find a tangible object in the vicinity of where you're reading this. Pick it up or place it near where you're sitting. Say or write down ten things about the item – if you pick up a book this could be something like 'this is a leather-bound book', 'it has twelve chapters', and 'it feels heavy in my hand'. Once you've made your ten observations about the item, do it all over again so you end up with twenty statements in total.

---

This exercise is called 10 × 2 and helps strengthen your observational skills by expanding the language you use when observing, making you more conscious of how you see the world around you, adding more nuance, and forcing you to delve deeper into what you see. If it's difficult to begin with to find twenty statements, it's OK to do 5 × 2 to begin with.

# A section for self-reflection

- Have you ever been in an interaction where you thought there was a disconnect between the other person's words and body language? What prevented you from exploring your observation?

- What do you think your own 'tells' are that might help others understand how you really feel?

- How would you like to use your improved observation skills at work?

# chapter 9

---

# Do you hear me? *(listening)*

I'm sure you're familiar with the expression 'hearing without lis-tening' about people who are doing the physical act of hearing the words spoken but who don't take in what's actually being said. To really listen to someone requires great communication skills. Where Chapter 8 focused on the ability to pay attention to what's going on around you, in this chapter I'll discuss the skill of listening to what's being said in a careful and active way. The two skills, observing and listening, complement each other and both are necessary for good communication: Most people who are good listeners are also good observers because in one sense observing is really just listening with the eyes, and it can add to the words being spoken and enhance the listener's understanding. This form of listening well – often called active or clean listening – isn't as easy as it sounds. The box below shows the key ingredients to develop good listening skills, each of which I'll go through in more detail.

## Key principles for listening well

- Be silent.
- 'Listen' to non-verbal cues (Chapter 8).
- Be curious.
- Be in the moment.
- Reserve judgement.

# Keeping schtum

In order to listen, we need to stop talking. It's impossible to listen well if we're the ones doing the talking or if we interrupt the person we're meant to be listening to – we're simply not able to listen properly as well as do the talking ourselves. Introverts tend to reflect on what's being said by default, leaving that extra space for the other person to take a breath and continue talking, or for them to stay silent to indicate they want input from us. Extroverts, on the other hand, see our silence as a green light to talk.[1] Over the years I've noticed that introverts often like to wait a beat after someone has finished talking, to make sure they're done and to avoid interrupting the original speaker. Extroverts start talking without this pause, not realising that introverts feel there should be one. This is one of the reasons why introverts find it hard to get a word in when extroverts are around. Introverts use the pause as a way to show respect for the other person, but this often isn't recognised by the extrovert who thinks we don't speak immediately because we're unsure of what to say or perhaps don't have a need to say anything at all. This leads to frustration – the introvert feels the extrovert is a selfish bulldozer, and the extrovert thinks the introvert doesn't have an opinion or is too meek to voice it, and so the bias against introverts perpetuates.[2]

Another common listening misunderstanding between extroverts and introverts is the level of interruption each is comfortable with. Introverts generally prefer to avoid interruption as we see it as a sign of rudeness, whereas extroverts often interrupt when they get excited about a topic and enjoy the interaction – they might not see that they're dominating the conversation in the process, and mistakenly assume that the introvert's silence means they don't have anything to contribute. Instead, the introvert will walk away from the conversation frustrated that their ideas weren't listened to and annoyed that the extrovert has such poor communication skills.[3] This is yet another example of what happens when we treat others as we would want to be treated, rather than how *they* want to be treated.

There are many misconceptions around listening that stem from not considering the introverted perspective. It's unfortunate that extroverts are rarely asked to talk less, as the bias of asking introverts instead to talk more perpetuates the pattern of poor communication.[4] It reduces the likelihood that listening skills improve and means that the best ideas won't be heard. Out of all the skills the quiet leader possesses, good listening is the one where the gap is the largest between the introvert and the extrovert.

---

## Benefits of listening well

- Obtains useful information.
- If others feel heard, they're more likely to listen to you back.
- Incorporating feedback from others increases adoption of your ideas.
- Creates space for others to share, and thereby generates connection.
- Shows others you care and therefore increases trust.
- Increases productivity and reduces less value-add activity.
- Increases team member engagement.

---

Karen, an insurance broker, shared with me a story about a manager of hers who only stopped to take a breath midway through sentences and never paused after a full stop, making it very difficult for anyone to contribute to a conversation without interrupting, which she wasn't comfortable with. To make matters worse, he would also share opinions as if they were fact, and assume that everyone in the room was in agreement without creating space for anyone to say otherwise, and refer to this 'agreement' in later meetings. We'll never know whether this was a result of poor communication skills or an intentional strategy, but it left Karen and her colleagues feeling like their manager wasn't interested in hearing their views. Over time they stopped attempting to make contributions, and they also ceased to object when he made assumptions about what they agreed with. This manager's behaviour was a result of them projecting their own view on to the team, and over time this had a detrimental impact; the organisation lost valuable input from experienced professionals and the manager in question missed out on useful feedback from his senior people. Ultimately the team were all also less bought into his ideas and felt less included than they would have been had they been given an opportunity to provide input.

In being silent we also allow others to hear what's **not** being said. If your friend tells you 'I'm really pleased with my new haircut' and you don't say anything, you're indicating that you disagree and might even find the haircut unflattering. Talking less can be powerful in other ways too: The silence generated from not talking can be uncomfortable for many, and often this means that the person you're talking to feels the need to fill the void and encourages them to share. Say you're talking to someone about rumours you've heard about an upcoming acquisition, and you'd like to know more; if you let your questions hang in the air, odds are your colleague will eventually add information they have, often more than they intended to, simply because the silence feels threatening to them. Equally, if you're requesting a volunteer for a task and nobody steps up immediately, someone will offer to help sooner or later if you stay silent. Sitting with the silence can initially feel uncomfortable if you're used to filling in any conversational lulls, but if you persevere the benefits are clear.[5]

It's an introvert strength to not need to be heard all the time.[6] When we meet new people, or in situations where we're unsure, we might worry that we'll be judged by the other person, and that we might not be taken seriously. Many therefore feel the need to talk first, in the subconscious hope that we'll signal that we know what we're talking about and that we're 'leaders' who take charge. As I mentioned in Chapter 2, whoever talks first will often set the tone and agenda for what will be discussed, and we subconsciously see those who talk more as dominant and (inaccurately) as more 'leader-like'. Knowing this, staying quiet feels like giving up an advantage – but actually we become more powerful when we show that we don't need to rely on these kinds of superficial (and temporary) interpersonal games.[7] Our ability to do this increases with the level of confidence we have, which I'll talk more about in the next chapter.

## Choose your moment

For all the reasons above, being silent is a crucial component of active listening,[8] but that doesn't mean that we should never speak up. It's important to find your voice, as staying silent all the time doesn't make you influential, nor does it make you a good quiet leader. Instead, we should aim to be actively silent – that is, have a clear purpose with our silence and know when it makes sense to use our voice. This could be when we want someone to stop talking as they're going on a bit without getting to the point and they're just talking for the sake of talking; if you want to insert your own argument in a discussion; or when you want to encourage others to speak when someone is dominating the conversation. The point with active listening isn't to always listen and never say anything; it's to be conscious about using your voice in the right way and at the right time, and about the impact it can have when you're intentional about how you use your silence.

Deciding when to be silent or speak isn't always clear-cut: Communication isn't always linear or a direct back and forth. Sometimes the best ideas come out of conversations that are messy and with no clear structure – they're ideas arising organically, not fully formed by anyone in the conversation but developed through the interaction itself. But that only works when everyone in the group is able to listen to the others and have the skills to build on each others' comments – what usually happens is that the loudest person takes over and everything builds on from that. It's been shown that the best approach to generate ideas from scratch isn't to put people in a room and ask them to brainstorm; it's far too easy to get stuck on a single path depending on where the conversation starts and who we listen to. I recently did a pub quiz where we had to identify the theme of the answers to ten different questions, and because one of these answers was 'yellow', as soon as one person suggested 'Easter' as the connecting theme, we simply weren't able to move away from Christianity so all other suggestions were around the theme of re-birth, which moved on to eggs, which moved on to chickens.[9] There are many books out there telling introverts how to get better at brainstorming, and how to speak up. What we should do instead is identify the best ways of achieving the outcome we want and educate ourselves on the creativity methods that do work – I bet we'd find that the more inclusive methods win since brainstorming isn't necessarily inclusive or creative.[10]

Staying silent doesn't need to be decided on spontaneously and is fortunately a skill that can be enhanced through practice. The exercise below (adapted from the In-Professional Development Institute) will help you be more conscious of how you approach your silence.

## Exercise

Imagine a work meeting you attended recently. You're going to re-create that meeting in your mind, with a focus on being intentional about your silence. Picture that you go into the meeting and that you want to focus on encouraging others to speak. In order to do this you need to break the usual pattern where you do most of the talking. Write down a sentence that you feel does this for you. What is the sentence? When I'm tired of hearing my own voice, I often use the expression 'round robin' with my team and ask them to provide updates on things top of their minds – sometimes they're concerns, sometimes they're things they want me to know. What opening question or request feels right for you?

Once you have your sentence, picture yourself saying it and imagine the types of responses you might get back. What other questions can you ask that encourage the other person to talk? Continue to note down the questions that encourage others to speak until you have a list you can leverage in future.

## Be curious

In conversations between introverts and extroverts, I've seen all too often that the louder party wants to engage but asks generic, superficial questions which the quieter person feels compelled to answer to avoid being rude, but then walks away from the interaction feeling like it was a waste of time. This arises because the two have different perspectives on what makes a good conversation; the introvert normally prefers to go deep to feel the conversation has meaning, and the extrovert prefers breadth. The quiet leader often feels that small talk of the generic, superficial kind is boring and prevents interpersonal connection, which is the opposite of how the extrovert sees a conversation, where any interaction is a gateway to a good relationship and that they are indeed getting to know you, even if they're really not.[11]

If you have a tendency to keep conversation at the superficial level and inadvertently create distance to others, reflect on the types of questions to ask to open the conversation up more – this can include asking about their personal motivations, backstories, asking questions you don't already know the answer to, and asking open-ended questions (not yes/no). In short, to be a good listener, you need to be curious about the other person.[12] This will then infuse your entire interaction – just asking one open-ended question isn't curiosity, but genuinely wanting to know about the other person will lead to additional follow-up questions based on what they respond.[13] Once we have curiosity about what the other person says, we open up the space for more active listening as it means we're less likely to think about what we're going to say next, what we'll have for dinner, or how we look in the dress we're wearing. In short, being curious is a vehicle for being more in the moment and focusing on the person or people in front of us.

---

## Examples of questions that support deeper dialogue

- What made you choose the career you're in?
- What's your favourite work-related memory?
- What's your greatest achievement?
- How do you start your day?
- What is the biggest challenge you're currently facing?
- Who in your career has influenced you the most and why?

---

# Be in the moment

Having your main focus on the other person is a key aspect of making them feel heard and seen.[14] The introvert is more likely to do this and reflect actively on what's being said, whereas the extrovert will assume that the silence is there to be filled, or to spend the period the other person talks to think of their own responses to – or their own anecdotes associated with – what's being said.[15] The ability to be present in the conversation is a major factor in both parties feeling that the interaction is a success. If you focus solely and intently on the person doing the talking, you'll generate a greater understanding of where they're coming from and what they're looking for, and you're in a position to show that you care. Ways to do this include asking follow-up questions, encouraging them to talk more using your own body language (such as eye contact or nodding your head), or just holding the space with them and allowing them to talk. We can sense when someone isn't fully engaged in a conversation, so by being present you also increase the trust between you, ultimately leading to you having more influence because they feel that you understand them.[16] The exercise below, a focused meditation, will help you stay in the moment for longer.[17] The mindfulness exercises in the previous chapters will also help you with this.

---

## Exercise

Sit comfortably, avoid hunching your back, and have your feet on the floor. You can also sit on the floor or on a meditation cushion. It's best if you're in a private space. Close your eyes and imagine an object, such as a candle, and focus on the item – look at the flickering flame, notice the colours of the flame and its movements, the candle holder shape, etc. Every time your mind wanders, notice it, make note of it and go back to visualising the object. If you find it difficult to stay alert while closing your eyes, you can also keep them open and resting softly on an object about 1–2 metres away from you. Doing this repeatedly for 5–10 minutes or longer (daily is recommended, but any effort will do) will over time help you to stay focused for longer without getting distracted.

---

Being distracted, such as looking at our phone, thinking about what we're going to say next, or following any other internal monologue, is the opposite of focusing on the other person and takes your attention away from being in the moment. This then has a detrimental effect on the relationship, your influence and your ability to achieve your objectives from the conversation – not to mention making it harder to remember what they said in the first place.

## Reserve judgement

Being a good listener also requires that we suspend a certain amount of judgement – that we try to understand where the other person is coming from rather than argue or deny the validity of their comments. This is difficult to do as it means temporarily setting aside our own views, and to resist being defensive, an intuitive human response when we hear something we disagree with or feel is unfair.[18] It helps to remember that letting the other person speak, and being interested in their views and how they're formed, doesn't automatically mean that we agree with the statements they're making.[19] A good place to start is to be curious about where the other person is coming from before responding – the key to this is in that pause that the introverts are so good at.

As a listener you interpret what the other person is saying and convert it into meaning. Your ability to understand what the speaker is intending to share can make or break the interaction. When we interpret, we run the risk of applying our own layer of meaning that the speaker might not have intended, and we always bring our own beliefs, values and assumptions to any interaction, which might result in you being defensive or disagreeing with the speaker unnecessarily. It's therefore important that we try to understand what the speaker had in mind and that our interpretation is as close to the speaker's intent as possible, though messages rarely get interpreted *exactly* as intended.[20] We can do this by listening to the words being spoken, paraphrasing what we hear to ensure we've understood correctly, or asking follow-up questions, but a good listener also uses more than the words – such as what they observe (see Chapter 8), the tone of voice, the context/purpose of the conversation, and what's not being said. Another useful listening skill is to refer back to the speaker's earlier statements to enhance understanding; for instance, you could identify contradictions or connect the dots for them using expressions such as 'earlier you said that. . . ' or 'how does that align with your earlier comment that. . . '.[21] All the different inputs you leverage – and a good listener will use them all – come together to help you interpret the conversation and form meaning.

Here's a personal example of how **not** to do this: I once had a colleague who had a habit of only picking out one part of what people were saying and missing the wider point being made. If I said 'I walked to the park near my house to get some fresh air at lunch as I felt really cooped up sitting in front of the laptop all day', his response wouldn't be to focus on the fact that I felt cooped up and needed fresh air, but he'd instead say something like 'you didn't go out at lunch, I saw you on Teams'. In his mind it was more important to correct the timing of the walk than attending to the intent behind the statement and the core message, which was about feeling cooped up. A better listener would have suspended judgement about the timing and instead focused on the need for fresh air, been curious about the impact of spending so much time by the computer, and considered the context that I was sharing a feeling and hadn't asked for a factual accuracy check.

Communication becomes problematic when we're not able to suspend judgement or we interpret incorrectly. But it's not easy to do this consistently. To see how difficult it can be, take a look at the box below which shows how many different variables there are in a single, simple sentence. Depending on the word you emphasise and which tone of voice you use, the statement takes on a different meaning entirely. These variables materially impact the interaction and can take the conversation in a multitude of different directions, which is why it's so important to be conscious about suspending judgement and to be curious about whether you've interpreted correctly.

## Exercise

The sentences below are identical. How does the meaning of the sentence change depending on which word you emphasise? How does it change if you adjust your tone of voice?

*Emphasis*

- I **will** meet you there.
- I will meet **you** there.
- I will meet you **there**.

*Tone of voice*

- What would the sentence sound like if you were angry?
- What would the sentence sound like if you were apologetic?

Approaching the conversation with a view to interpret as accurately as possible is a great starting point and helps you better understand the perspective of the other person. Once you have that, you can decide whether it's appropriate to provide your own views or help with solutions or recommendations should these be needed. None of these (which are judgement-based) are part of the initial step of the interaction, which is all about listening actively to understand the other person.[22] When you focus solely on the other person and stay in the present, when you understand the intent and purpose of their words, and approach the interaction with curiosity and suspend judgement, you have the ingredients of good listening. You might not, however, always find it easy to receive the messages you hear, and that's when confidence and humility, empathy and calmness are needed. These are all also perhaps surprising strengths of the quiet leader and the focus of the next few chapters.

# A section for self-reflection

- - - - - - - - - - - - - - - - - - - - - - - - - - - - - - - - - - - - - -

- When have you felt really heard? What did the other person say and do to make you feel that way?

- Is there anyone whose ability to listen – to be silent at the right moments, to encourage others to talk, suspend judgement, be in the moment and stay curious – that you're impressed by? What in their approach can you emulate?

- Are there people in your workplace that you feel misunderstand you more often than others? What can be going on in your interactions with them to cause this?

- - - - - - - - - - - - - - - - - - - - - - - - - - - - - - - - - - - - - -

# chapter 10

---

# Eating humble pie
*(humility)*

I once sang in a choir where the musical director James told us all to be 'strong and wrong.' We were an enthusiastic group, though not very keen on rehearsing, and the quality of output reflected that: We showed up consistently, but most of us (with some honourable exceptions!) were generally unprepared. Because we were all very self-aware about our less-than-amazing harmonies, we ended up also singing rather quietly even when the songs needed us to be loud. James therefore wanted us to move past our inhibitions and sing loudly even if we weren't really sure what we were doing – hence 'strong and wrong'. It was a great way to get us to care less about a wrong note or incorrect lyric here and there, and worked wonders for our small group of amateur indie folk singers. In the business world, you'd think companies would want to avoid 'strong and wrong' since it could lead to all sorts of chaos – inaccurate financial statements, misleading press releases, foolish acquisitions, lawsuits and regulatory fines, and a company might ultimately go bust. Despite these material consequences, strong and wrong is actually often the norm. This is because most organisations miss emphasis on a key skill: Humility.

A key component of humility is the ability to admit when you're wrong and to acknowledge that you alone don't have all the answers, recognising that you're neither perfect nor omniscient. We all have things to learn and can always do better, and quiet leaders recognise this more than most.[1] Just like my choir realised that we're not the greatest group of singers alive, humility leads to a willingness to be challenged and receive feedback, and an openness to try new things. It also means you're more aware of your limitations. Humble leaders don't like to talk about their own accomplishments (a very introvert attribute[2]) – and yet it's this very trait, the focus on the end result for the organisation and not on inflating our own ego, that makes organisations led by humble leaders so successful.[3]

Of all the elements that make up humility (summarised in the box below), there's one fundamental requirement: Given the need to recognise your own fallibility and being open to others' views, being a humble leader means you have to be very comfortable in your own skin. Being humble requires heaps of confidence.

---

### Key aspects of humility

- Requires having true, inner confidence.
- Be open to challenge and inputs from others.
- Be open to feedback (additional content also in Chapter 7).
- Acknowledge your limitations (covered in Chapter 7).
- Accept when you're wrong.

---

## Certainty and conviction, competence and confidence

In Chapter 2, I talked about the mental shortcuts we use to determine leadership ability, which help our brains navigate the hierarchy of our social environment and cause us to often mistake loudness, certainty and conviction for confidence and competence. Inner confidence, however, is different to the loud, self-aggrandising type of confidence that we often let ourselves be fooled by. Inner confidence is a quiet skill – it's calm, composed and doesn't care what others think. Introverts develop this because we often lack recognition from the outside so we have to have deep trust in ourselves coming from within.[4] This kind of confidence has sometimes recently also been called 'happy high status'[5] – someone so comfortable in their own skin they don't need validation from anyone else. Humility requires this type of inner confidence to make you as a leader able to hear what others have to say and take onboard useful input, to make you better without letting it throw you off course and affect your ability to persevere towards your goals.[6] Humility without inner confidence is just constant doubt, which would make you ineffective as a leader, and self-aggrandising confidence without humility is a short step away from hubris, which isn't leadership at all. Both come from a place of insecurity.

Consider the following examples: Caroline is a hard-working quiet leader working as head of department at a London primary school. She's worked with her manager for several years, prior to which they were peers. Before he got the role as her manager he headed up his own department, and at the time Caroline made a suggestion about his course content, intended to improve the offering to the students. He didn't appreciate the feedback, and when he became her manager, Caroline told me how he on several occasions referred to her earlier feedback to him – several years later! Similarly, spare a thought for Michael, who had to sit through a vitriol from his manager about a candidate for a team lead position: The manager had asked the candidate to apply and they were clearly the favourite, but for personal reasons decided to withdraw during the interview process. The manager felt personally slighted at this and spoke negatively of the candidate in a team meeting in front of Michael and his peers, saying they wouldn't have been offered the job anyway.

The behaviours leaking from Caroline and Michael's managers aren't the actions of leaders with strong inner confidence – the most important thing to them was to preserve their self-image causing them to lash out, leaking their hidden insecurities.

In contrast, consider someone who has true inner confidence: Imagine George Clooney at a drinks reception. He's chatting away to another famous actor, wearing a dapper black evening suit with a crisp white shirt and a black tie. He's having a great time when someone walks up to him, taps him on the shoulder and asks him to bring them a drink. Being mistaken for a waiter would probably make most of us feel slightly self-conscious, feeling awkward both for ourselves and the other person at the same time. George, though, just laughs, confirms the order and proceeds to get the drink delivered.[7] Even if this anecdote isn't true (which allegedly it is), it shows exactly the type of behaviour someone with strong inner confidence exhibits: They don't take anything personally and everything they do seems easy and natural.

## Exercise

Try to understand if your own humility is based on confidence or insecurity by considering a recent interaction where you believe you reacted with humility. Ask yourself: Did what I say indicate that I truly believe I'm good enough at what I do? If not, what areas do my doubts focus on? Where does this doubt come from?

# The impact of culture

Many organisations misunderstand this concept of inner confidence. They mistake humility for submissiveness, and being open to others' opinions, as introverts often are, is seen as lacking the courage of your convictions.[8] In these organisations, to ask questions is to be meek, which impacts a leader's career prospects, and they define a good leader as someone who never doubts themselves. Most quiet leaders I've spoken to, however, are neither submissive nor lacking in self-belief – it's simply how their environment misinterprets the signals they send out. I once had a conversation with a colleague where I told him 'I don't compete with anyone'. By this, I meant that I don't see the value in competing because comparison is not where I draw my confidence from, which I thought was obvious. My colleague's response was 'don't put yourself down' – he'd misinterpreted my statement as an expression of low self-belief. These misunderstandings perpetuate how we're seen as introverts. There are different types of humility that impact this impression. For instance, if someone praises you for a job well done, an introvert might say 'Oh it's nothing' because it genuinely wasn't a lot of effort on their part – the good quality came naturally. This is self-abasing humility and could be seen as a reflection of low confidence. Similarly, some leaders apply something called 'attunement' where they tune in to the psychological state of the person they're talking to – for instance they might tone down their dominance – to create rapport.[9] This isn't a category of humility, but can often be mistaken for low confidence, when in fact it's a conscious decision to improve an interpersonal relationship. If others often think you have low confidence (and this doesn't match how you feel inside), I recommend avoiding attunement behaviours until you're sure your internal quiet self-confidence isn't misinterpreted in that environment. However, if you're a generally dominant individual wanting to practice humility, attunement is a great tool to build better relationships where you come across as less forceful and give more space to others. There's another type, appreciative humility, which can only be interpreted as strength. An example is saying 'Well done on the promotion!' to a colleague, showing appreciation and celebrating their success.[10] For introverts and extroverts alike, it's a safe form of humility rarely misinterpreted.

## Exercise

Think of a recent situation where you felt humbled; perhaps someone pointed out a mistake you made. How do you think your response communicated your level of confidence? How did you feel? If there's a disconnect between what you communicated and how you felt, could you have expressed yourself differently to better align the feeling with the interpretation?

| Humility and relationship dynamics | | |
| --- | --- | --- |
| *Example* | *Category* | *Explanation* |
| I couldn't have done it without you | Self-abasing humility | Low confidence. Putting yourself down by saying the only reason you succeeded was because of the other person |
| Great presentation, you're so good at public speaking (you could even say they're better than you) | Appreciative humility | Positive self-image. Not putting yourself down or saying you're not good, but recognising that someone is better in a particular area |
| I failed on that exam too | Attunement (often mistaken for self-abasing humility, though not a humility type as such) | Neutral or negative view depending on listener. Speaker is showing that you have had the same experience as the other person and putting yourself in the same boat as them |

# Being open to challenge and input

We live in a complex world, facing complex problems. The humble leader recognises this and knows – and isn't afraid to say – that they don't have all the answers. They're therefore more likely to openly request input from a multitude of others since they know that groups are better able to solve complex problems than individuals alone. Introverts are particularly good at this because they're not threatened by others and are more comfortable with the concept of 'sharing leadership', meaning they give others the spotlight, actively listen to what others have to say, give credit where this is due and make sure theirs isn't the only voice to be heard.[11] In this kind of environment, the leader is hard to spot, but this suits the introvert well as they don't need to be the centre of attention all the time.[12] This type of environment works well for an employee who actively makes suggestions and looks for ways of doing things better. Research has shown that introvert leaders and this kind of proactive employee together outperform teams led by extroverts. This happens because the quiet leader is better at listening and actively seeks input and – crucially – implements the suggestions they receive. This in turn encourages more good ideas, which leads the team to share more, in a virtuous cycle.[13]

This, however, shouldn't be interpreted to mean that quiet leaders don't believe in their own ideas or that others are always right – they're simply humble enough to realise that in today's dynamic world it's possible there's a perspective they've missed – they're not so invested in their own ideas that they hang on to them unnecessarily, and they recognise that with more inputs the solution is more likely to be successful.[14] This leader is very clear on what they know and what they don't know – and they only operate within their 'circle of competence', confident enough to accept what they don't know and not be ashamed of it.[15]

As a way to encourage input from others, you might think that asking questions is a good place to start, and as I described in Chapter 9, being genuinely curious and creating space for others to contribute shows your colleagues that you really want to hear from them. This comes naturally to introverts.[16] In some organisations, however, asking questions is seen as meek and submissive.[17] We should therefore use questions carefully. Asking 'Should we introduce this as a new product?' indicates less certainty than 'I think we should introduce this as a new product. What do you think?'. There's also a psychological dimension to consider – when you state your preference before asking the question, you might be influencing those around you more than you think, especially if you have power in the relationship. We should therefore use this approach with caution. An alternative in this scenario is to state that you have an opinion but would like to hear others' views first. Similarly, a question can also be a threat: 'Why hasn't the Anderson acquisition completed?' could be interpreted to mean you feel progress is too slow. If instead you ask 'What do we need for the Anderson account to complete?' you're still signalling that you'd like progress, but also that there are gaps in your knowledge that you need input on and that you're there to help.[18] I've included a list of example questions in the box below – they're all neutrally worded and open-ended (not closed yes/no questions), which encourages a more elaborate response from the other person.

## Types of questions to show you genuinely want to hear from others

- What would you like me to change about [insert situation]?
- What is your biggest frustration?
- What can I do to help?
- How do you see this play out?
- What are the biggest challenges you anticipate?

## Exercise

Picture yourself discussing with your team. In addition to the suggestions in the box above, what other questions can you think of to encourage openness? Write these down. Wait a few minutes, then go back and re-read your questions – this time from your team's perspective. Can they be misinterpreted? If so, rewrite them until they are less threatening and don't include too much of your own view.

## Accept when you're wrong

Just like one person can't have all the answers, you might also not get every decision right every time. When mistakes happen, the quiet leader owns the situation and doesn't hesitate to highlight that they're wrong – and takes steps to fix it. Being vocal about errors helps create a culture where it's OK for others to be wrong, increases psychological safety and leads to an environment where it's possible to innovate and experiment, ultimately generating higher performance. To accept when you're wrong means to acknowledge the error to yourself as well as to those around you. This shouldn't be done half-heartedly as it'll be clear you don't really mean it. If you say 'I'm so annoyed at myself for this, I got it wrong and I'll make the change first thing in the morning', that's a human response, it focuses on you ('I') as the person making the mistake and takes responsibility (you're not trying to shift blame) and makes a commitment to correct it. Similarly, saying 'I got these numbers wrong – you were right' creates that same accountability while also giving credit. To accept if you're wrong also means to not kick yourself too much, especially in front of others – you're human, after all. This can be hard to do as it's natural to want to show that getting it wrong isn't typical for you. However, self-flagellation makes it harder for your team to acknowledge their own mistakes as they know how badly you'll take it. Being transparent about the error, stating that you're in the wrong and explaining the steps you'll take to correct it (and then doing them) are the only things needed.

## Exercise

Think of a mistake you've made recently. Did you handle this as a humble, quiet leader or as an insecure individual? How would you have owned up to it differently if you had a do-over?

There are only four steps to it, but the transparency and succinctness can be hard, so be wary of fake humility: I once had a manager who thought he was humble because he'd apologise when he was wrong – but only when the impact was limited and the error was inconsequential. For the big mistakes, he'd ignore the mistake, blame others, or blame circumstance, never himself. In some instances, leaders like this have learnt from the environment they're in; if the archetype of a good leader is the person who never doubts themselves, it's difficult to admit to a mistake. You'd be going against the corporate ideal and potentially hurting your own career prospects if you were transparent about your own errors. Unfortunately, this leads to people pretending that they're something they're not, leaving no room for learning and growth.[19] It's not impossible that as a quiet leader your instincts are right but your environment is wrong for you. Two of the senior leaders I interviewed for this book noted that they only got comfortable with their quiet style once they found organisations that supported them being themselves – for most it takes years of trial and error to understand that there's nothing wrong with us, and to get rid of the doubt that comes from not being in the default 'in-group'.

## When leaders who aren't humble make mistakes

They:

- Blame others
- Minimise the problem

- Try to hide the mistake
- Don't give credit if others were right
- Get defensive
- Make no commitments to fix the problem
- Don't commit to avoiding the mistake in future

## Be open to feedback

You probably think you're approachable and that your team feel they can come to you with any concerns. That might be true, but it's more likely that your team sees you differently from how you see yourself. I explained in Chapter 7 that others can usually see us more accurately than we see ourselves, and self-reflection on our own abilities from a varied range of sources is a useful way to develop humility. It's therefore key that you get perspectives from others, but this isn't easy to do. A study by psychologists Rosen and Tesser[20] showed that people hesitate when asked to share bad news, even with strangers. Their study included research participants who thought they were in a holding area to participate in a study on deodorants, and while waiting to be called the researchers entered and asked them 'Are you Glen Lester?' (Gwen for women) – which of course they weren't – and that they had news from home for him/her. Could they please pass the message on to Glen if they saw him? Participants were in two groups – some received good news about Glen's family, and others received bad news. When the real Glen subsequently arrived, more than half passed on the message when they had good news to share – five times as many as when the news was bad. Eighty per cent of the bad news group refused to share anything even when prompted by Glen! The people you want feedback from might be too intimidated by you, worried about how you'll react if they tell you what they really think, or they might just be too nice.[21] Feedback at work is especially rare as it's so much easier for people to talk about you to others instead of directly to you. There are certain things we can do to increase the chance that we'll hear the unvarnished truth, however, and I've outlined these in the box below.[22]

---

## How to increase likelihood of honest feedback

- Remind them that they're doing you a favour (and mean it!).

- Focus on future behaviour. If you ask about a specific situation from the past people are less likely to feel they're helping and more likely to feel they're criticising, which as humans we do want to temper (it feels like conflict, which most of us want to avoid).

- Don't just ask the question once, prompt for additional input and ask follow-up questions if you'd like to know more.

- Listen without judgement – don't provide justification or explanation for why you did what you did, it will sound defensive. This is hard as you want them to see **your** reality, but ultimately it's **their** reality you're looking for and not persuading them of yours.

- Write down the responses. This helps to show that you're taking their feedback seriously, and it also creates a pause so they can think of additional, useful input.

- Thank them for their honesty, which makes them more likely to continue it in future.

---

Not only are we inherently hesitant to deliver negative messages to others; it's also difficult to proactively ask for them. I once had a manager who prided himself on being open to feedback, but in the years I worked for him he only asked for it once – and that was at the end of one of my performance reviews, 5 minutes before the end of the meeting. Suffice to say, I didn't get the impression he had genuine interest in hearing his team's views. To ask for feedback requires humility, and hearing what others think is almost certainly going to make you more humble in turn. It's easier to hear harsh truths if we think of the feedback as a gift – one that makes you better – but that doesn't mean it'll be easy to hear or delivered in the way you prefer. The other person might use words you disagree with or a tone you don't appreciate. If you're able to see past all of this, which is easier if you're secure in your own value, you can then find the gold nuggets within their message. You don't need to take onboard everything they say, you don't need to make any changes as a result if you don't want to, but just knowing what their reality is and how they see you is always going to be valuable.

## Exercise

Consider a difficult piece of feedback you've received, recently or from the more distant past. Why has this feedback stayed with you? What is it about this feedback that feels difficult? Why do you think this resistance exists?

# A section for self-reflection

- Which individual seems humble yet powerful to you? What is it about their behaviour that gives you this impression and what can you learn from them?

- Which component of humility is hardest for you to model? Why do you think this is?

- Have there been situations where you felt confident but your humility was misinterpreted by those around you? Why do you think this happened?

# chapter 11

---

# I feel you
# (empathy)

So far I've discussed individual skills that, although related, are distinct from each other. This chapter is a bit different in that empathy is built on multiple introvert strengths which I've already covered. Empathy, simply put, is our ability to put ourselves in other people's shoes and is one of the most important skills in business today, and it drives higher levels of performance.[1] Empathy comes, firstly, from picking up other people's cues through observation and active listening (Chapters 8 and 9). Listening helps because it gives you the ability to better understand other people's unique situation,[2] and attention to non-verbal cues from observation is an essential part of that understanding.[3] Secondly, empathy requires humility (Chapter 10) so we don't assume we know everything about how someone else feels. Finally, it requires self-awareness (Chapter 7) because it's easier to understand others if we understand ourselves.[4] This chapter therefore builds on the content in those chapters, and helps introverts maintain strong interpersonal relationships with colleagues and customers alike.

Empathy is often conflated with sympathy, but the two are different in intent, how they affect our relationships and in outcome: If you show someone sympathy there's an element of sadness and distance attached to it – if you have sympathy for someone who's recently lost a relative, you feel sorry for them and hope their grief is manageable. Empathy, on the other hand, is feeling the loss with them, either because you're able to understand it intellectually (called cognitive empathy or perspective-taking), or because you've felt it yourself previously, called emotional empathy.[5] The word comes from Greek and combines the words 'feeling' and 'into others', so empathy literally means sharing another person's feeling.[6] While a good quiet leader will do this in a way that models empathy for others, feeling what others might feel isn't something that comes easily to everyone; those with dominant personalities, such as someone very competitive or aggressive, have more work to do before it becomes a habit (for more on dominant personalities, see Chapter 2).[7]

Whichever group you sit in, empathy without action has merit if it makes you better able to understand what others are going through, but understanding without action only takes us so far. The researcher Paul Ekman identified a third type, in addition to cognitive and emotional empathy, called **compassionate** empathy. This is the kind that drives us to act.[8] (You might recall that Ekman was the guy behind the science applied in the TV show *Lie to Me*, which I mentioned in Chapter 8. I recommend both his book *Emotions Revealed* as well as Paul Gibsons's *The Compassionate Mind* for more details on empathy.) It's this action and interaction with others that makes empathy such a crucial element of high-performing teams. So if this doesn't come as easily to you as it does to an introvert, or you'd like to get even better, what can you do about it?

# A bit of science

Empathy appears to be an instinct as well as a skill, unique to humans.[9] If you sit next to a hungry person and are offered a nice meal for you both, not many would only accept the meal for themselves – even when there's no chance of social penalty later. Studies using monkeys, however, show that they don't share this instinct; given the choice of pressing one of two levers – one that offers food for both themselves and the other monkey, and one that only feeds themselves – the monkey's choice is random.[10] Humans seem to have an in-built mechanism for fairness (what researchers call 'pro-sociality'); we even refuse free money if we don't feel the allocation is fair.[11] Imagine that someone gives you £10 but you have to give some of it to a stranger. How much would you give? In theory, a penny is enough since the stranger would be better off than they were before. Consistently, however, when this experiment is run, we offer on average 25 per cent to the other person. Scientists believe this is down to our mirror neuron system, the part of us that motivates compassionate behaviour, and is driven by empathy. It's the part of you that flinches if you see someone cut themselves – you can imagine how it feels, so your body is 'mirroring' the experience. This increases the likelihood that you act in a compassionate way towards the person who's cut themselves; perhaps you offer them a plaster or call 999.[12] This all happens in the middle prefrontal part of the brain, in an area called the insula.[13] Information such as heart rate, muscle tension and speed of breathing goes around the body and up through the insula to the prefrontal cortex to tell us how to feel.[14] This is why knowing our own bodies and being self-aware increases our ability for empathy, and as we know from Chapter 2, the introvert has higher levels of blood flow in the prefrontal cortex, so this area is more active in the introvert's brain to begin with.

Studies and MRI scans have shown that the anterior insula is activated when we see others in pain.[15] They also show that people who meditate have a higher level of insula activation when seeing others in pain than those who don't meditate.[16] While cause and effect is always hard to establish, it won't hurt to practice a meditation technique called 'loving-kindness' if you'd like to increase your empathy levels. There are a lot of variations of this technique available, but I've outlined an example below to get you started.[17]

## Exercise

Sit in a quiet place and think of a person you like and care about. Repeat the following:

- May you be happy.
- May you be healthy.
- May you be well.
- May you be safe.
- May you be at peace.

Then do the same picturing a stranger, and finally a third time with someone you have a fraught relationship with. Ideally you'll do this exercise with closed eyes, but if you have them open, keep a soft gaze looking into the distance. If you find this exercise hard to begin with, start with the person close to you and repeat until you're ready to expand the compassion circle. Always do the difficult individual last.

While the insula is responsible for care and has to be in the **on** mode, the brain circuitry for anger and retaliation also plays a part and also needs to be switched **off**, since it reduces our ability to feel others' pain.[18] Scientists have found that to do this, we need to reduce the connection (the strength of the neural routes the brain signals take) between the prefrontal cortex and the amygdala. There's not a lot of research on how to do this, but I've included below a suggestion from psychologists Davidson and Begley. Their belief is that focusing on suffering will lead to sustained activation of the insula, amygdala and anterior cingulate cortex, strengthening the neural routes relating to distress to make them stronger than those relating to anger.[19]

## Exercise

Sit in a comfortable position. Close your eyes and visualise someone suffering – if you don't have anyone in your immediate circle this applies to, you can instead think about a generic person's suffering, such as a child with cancer, or a refugee escaping from their native country. Spend 5 minutes considering their plight, how it might feel, the impact the situation has on their family and loved ones, and what might happen to them. Breathe in as you think about them and feel their suffering wrapped around you and going into your body. On the out-breath, imagine the warmth of your care and compassion flowing towards them.

Research shows that the insula is key for empathy; however, we also know that hormones play a role. Our ability to feel empathy is temporarily reduced when we're stressed, which releases a hormone called cortisol. Reducing cortisol levels can therefore enable an increase in our feelings of empathy, and this can be done by promoting production of oxytocin, sometimes called the 'love hormone'. Simply put, oxytocin is the hormone produced when a woman gazes into the eyes of her newborn child or when we touch a romantic partner. It works for strangers too: One study showed that spraying artificial oxytocin into participants' noses increased their donations to charity. The only problem is that oxytocin comes with bias: I mentioned in Chapter 2 that we treat people differently depending on whether we consider them part of our own group (the 'in-group'). This bias is relevant for empathy, as it turns out we're more empathetic towards people from our own in-group.[20] If we're not aware of this, strengthening our empathy muscles will only improve interactions with *some* of those we interact with, which as a leader is the last thing you want to be doing (especially since introverts often find ourselves being in the out-group to begin with).

# Widening our circle of concern

The reason we treat people from the out-group less preferentially is simply because they're different to us, and we find it harder to identify with people who aren't the same as us. Seeing their different perspective is harder still. Seeing someone as 'not like us' means we're less likely to feel empathy with them and less likely to help, a concept known as parochial altruism.[21] We don't do this consciously, but we might rationalise that our colleague Emma's mental health fundraiser needs our donation more than a refugee charity does – perhaps we tell ourselves that the charity receives enough support already, or that our money will make a bigger difference to Emma's cause – and as a result we suppress our empathy through logic. This tendency can be intentionally amplified to strengthen relationships – sports teams do this all the time. In *Messengers*, Martin and Marks recount the results of a study taking place at a Manchester United game, football fans being known for having strong bonds with each other: Fans were walking around the stadium when they observed a jogger tripping over (this was actually a member of the research team, pretending to fall). The fans were less likely to offer help if the jogger was wearing a shirt of the opposing team or a neutral colour (30 per cent offered), than they were if he wore a Manchester United shirt (85 per cent). This effect fell away if the fans had previously been primed to think of themselves as fans of football first, and team second.[22] This changed the in- and out-groups for them, and they considered what they had in common with the other team (a love of football) more than what separated them (supporting different teams). This in- and out-group tendency means our empathy has a narrow focus and comes with restrictions, which isn't the universal empathy we need for improved team performance (unless we think of the whole organisation as the team). In the words of Barack Obama, we should 'widen our circle of concern'.[23]

One way to do this is to increase interaction; once we get to know people as individuals, we start to see more and more the things we have in common before we see the things that separate us. Increased empathy follows.[24] One global conglomerate has introduced 'well-being sessions', open to all employees, where participants discuss sensitive topics and share personal troubles. Someone might talk about the loss of a parent, or another their concerns about burnout. Those with similar experiences offer help, listen or make suggestions for how to tackle the problem. These sessions have the effect that individuals across teams and geographies get to know each other better and see colleagues as humans first – with unique life experiences, but shared struggles nonetheless – and belonging to a particular department second. Ultimately this changes the corporate culture as more and more participate, and people feel they can be vulnerable at work. Even if you don't have this available in your organisation (maybe you could set one up?), you can practice what it's like to take another person's perspective.

## Exercise

Think about a recent conflict with someone, such as a colleague. Write about the episode as if you were someone not involved with it but wanted the best for both parties involved. Write from a third-party perspective, using he/she/they pronouns.

## The business case

What helped for the well-being sessions above was that people approached them with an open mind and curiosity – and curiosity is a key starting point for empathy to flourish. However, true empathy is also about appreciating the differences between us – to have empathy *despite* our differences. For this we need not just curiosity, but also to show respect for others' feelings, pause judgement when their views are different to our own and respond to what they share with us in a way they recognise and understand. For instance, I'm very bad at remembering specifics such as pet or children's names – I remember the content of what's shared and the emotions attached, and I like to think I'm supportive, but for some reason names are hard. I've found it best to be open about this and explain that my lack of memory for names doesn't mean that I don't care, and that my way of having empathy isn't to memorise facts, but rather doing my bit to create an environment where everyone can thrive, such as encourage challenge, give everyone a voice and understand what makes each individual tick.

There's empirical evidence for this approach: Empathy makes people feel understood, and when we feel understood we feel more included and respected for who we are.[25] In this environment, people are more likely to trust that you have their best interests at heart and are therefore more willing to follow your lead. Research has shown that empathy improves mood, and mood affects performance; when teams are feeling positive, they communicate more openly, collaborate better and have fewer conflicts. With these components in place, teams execute more successfully.[26] As their leader, getting to know each person individually puts you in a position to understand their uniqueness; you're attuned to what they want, what worries they have, and what motivates them. These are the things that create warmth. To be effective and build sustainable relationships with others – which is needed in any leadership role – there needs to be a certain level of this.[27] For the avoidance of doubt, this doesn't mean anything goes; empathy isn't a free pass for everyone to do whatever they like and expect understanding.[28] To show empathy doesn't mean we understand why someone is a low performer and then do nothing; it simply means that we let them know they're not performing in a way that recognises how it would feel for them to hear that message and help them improve if they can (otherwise, help them find a new role). As I mentioned in Chapter 10, feedback is a kindness and everyone deserves to hear what can make them better, delivered with empathy (the theoretical feedback model used is secondary – I'm sure we've all been trained in a number of different ones and been told to avoid the feedback sandwich).

I recognise that I might be delusional in thinking I've been successful at showing empathy in ways that resonate with my teams. Research shows that the more senior you become, the lower your ability to be empathetic[29] and you're also more likely to overestimate your own ability to empathise, an unfortunate combination[30] (read Chapter 7 for ways to increase your self-awareness!). A 2014 study showed that managers had lower activity in the part of the brain associated with taking the perspective of others, as we know a key component of empathy, and in fact some saw other human being as commodities, like pawns to be moved around at will[31] (terms such as Human Resources are not helping this). This is a form of 'dehumanisation', which – although less extreme – is similar in nature to what soldiers use in battle: Seeing others as 'non-human' appears to suppress empathy and makes it easier to create emotional distance to perform difficult decisions, such as letting someone go or giving a bad performance review.[32] Of course, although the emotionally draining tasks of being a leader might be easier with less empathy, we know that this dehumanising process leads to lower performance than in teams where leadership empathy levels are high. To check your own current perspective-taking levels, complete the exercise below – it's intended to be used on others, not on yourself, so it will work best if you get someone else to give you the instructions.[33]

## Exercise

Snap your fingers five times as quickly as you can, with your dominant hand. Find a pen and draw a capital E on your forehead. The person reading this out to you can then tell you if it looks like illustration 1 or 2.

Illustration 1: You easily take the perspective of others, a key element of empathy.

Illustration 2: You find perspective-taking more challenging and have some work to do before empathy comes naturally to you.

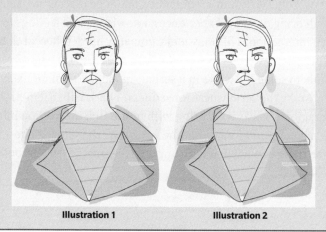

**Illustration 1**　　　　　**Illustration 2**

# Avoiding the pitfalls

In addition to the in- and out-group differences and the risk of thinking you're more empathetic than you are, there are other empathy dangers to be aware of.

- **Burnout:** Empathy comes at a cost. If you feel what others feel too strongly or too often, you'll have more of the stress hormone cortisol in your body. This exposure can lead to burnout.[34] It's almost as if empaths have a thinner line between the negative experiences of others and their own feelings. This is why doctors, while they need good bedside manners, take care to not get too close to patients as it affects their own well-being in the long run. If we empathise too much, we almost lose our own feelings in the process; in the words of David Siegel, Clinical Professor of Psychiatry at UCLA, we need to 'remain differentiated'.[35] We saw this materialise during the COVID-19 pandemic, where health professionals faced such high patient volumes and felt such a high level of personal responsibility that they were unable to protect themselves to the same extent as they would under more normal circumstances.

- **Projection:** I've said that empathy is being able to feel what others are feeling – but we can only know what they feel if they tell us. Otherwise, our assumptions might be inaccurate, since we all bring our own experiences, knowledge and feelings to each interaction. This may make empathy harder. Research has shown that if we talk to someone who's sad and then move on to talk to someone who's in a serious mood, we're more likely to mistake the seriousness for sadness. This is called 'emotional contagion' – it's as if we bring with us the first interaction into the next one and forget that the two aren't the same.[36] The same thing can happen with our own feelings; if I'm nervous about an upcoming event and my partner is uncharacteristically quiet during dinner that evening, I'm more likely to assume that he's nervous about something too – but he might just be contemplating the route he's going to take for his bike ride the next day. For empathy to flourish (and for all the other reasons mentioned previously in this book), it's therefore important that we don't make assumptions in our interactions.

Assumptions affect our thoughts about what others need from us, too – and how we react: If you hear your front door slam as your teenager returns home, your response might be that they've had a bad day and they need to vent – but if you know it's windy outside, you might instead assume the door got caught in the draught and go to close the garden door that's also open.

Empathy is an interpersonal skill and like all skills requires work – to imagine the other person's perspective, consider it, to look inside ourselves and be motivated to engage. The framework below can be helpful to have in your back pocket as you experiment with real-world examples.[37] As you do, remember that it's unlikely to always go to plan. As things get difficult, keep trying and stay calm; and fortunately, calmness is the final of the seven quiet leader skills.

## Exercise

Consider a situation you want to understand better, for instance a conflict or an interaction you felt puzzled by. Fill in each section in the image below with this person and interaction in mind. This is called an empathy map and helps you see the other person's perspective from multiple angles.

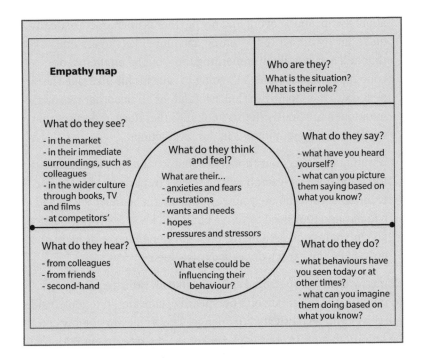

# A section for self-reflection

- - - - - - - - - - - - - - - - - - - - - - - - - - - - - - - - - - - -

- How open are you at work about feelings? How do you think this affects your team?

- How does it make you feel when others display feelings? How do you tend to respond?

- What can you do to enhance empathy in your workplace?

- - - - - - - - - - - - - - - - - - - - - - - - - - - - - - - - - - - -

# chapter 12

---

# Keep calm and carry on (*calmness*)

In this final chapter, I'll bring all of the quiet leader's skills together in one word: Calmness. Whether we reflect on feedback we receive, observe the world around us, assess ourselves in a self-aware fashion, whether we listen to others and encourage challenge, or try to understand our surroundings better, on our best days we do so with a calm, grounded energy and a quiet confidence, the epitome of a good leader.[1] Calmness in this sense isn't exterior-only, a duck on a river with a quiet demeanour above water, paddling furiously underneath. Calmness is indeed about the environment you create and how you come across to those around you, but crucially it's also an inner calmness; a duck gliding effortlessly on the water, calm both above *and* below. It's been said that verbal expression is the mirror of the mind[2] – in other words, what you say and how you say it reflects what goes on inside. Extroverts might feel that a focus on internal calmness advocates for internalising of problems in an unhealthy way,[3] but being and staying calm isn't about suppressing anything; it's about finding ways to respond and tackle issues head on in a way that keeps the room temperature at a suitable level.

The quiet leader provides reassurance for those around. Think of a fire where everyone's running around looking for a bucket of water, and the quiet leader purposefully stops, looks around to find the button that will activate the sprinklers across the whole floor, and with one firm press on the alarm solves the problem. They exude a calm energy that says 'it's going to be okay'.[4] Calm doesn't mean holding back or hesitating,[5] it means taking up the space required to express yourself in an assertive yet low-key manner. It's stating firmly 'I won't be able to do that' when someone asks something you're not willing or have time to do, instead of a frantic and frustrated 'Can't someone else help around here?!'

If you feel calm most of the time that's great – most of us do when things are going well – but it's harder to stay calm when we're stressed, and therein lies the challenge. The more we can practice the muscles that help us stay calm, when we're already calm, the more effective they'll be.

# Feeling it

Many organisations are financially stretched, face rising costs, often have high regulatory pressure and fast-moving consumer preferences and expectations, with reputational damage only an unfortunate keystroke away. In this environment, it's understandable that many leaders slide into a 'productivity first' focus, expecting employees to ignore their feelings and crack on with delivery (we can feel things in our spare time!). But we're all human, and if we don't provide an outlet for inevitable emotions, they'll leak out anyway, usually in unhealthy ways, either in an interaction with an innocent colleague or customer, or later on that evening with our spouse. I'm sure you've noticed how annoying it is when someone tells you to 'calm down' – making you anything but calm. What I'm advocating isn't that we shouldn't feel at all – that's impossible for all humans – and I'm not a proponent of artificial suppression of feelings, but rather that we enhance our ability to handle stress when it occurs.

We do this by noticing feelings when they arise, noticing our own observation with detached curiosity ('oh, I feel tense, where's that coming from?') and then move on from them or consciously choose how to take action if that's appropriate. I usually picture emotions wash over my legs as if I'm in a river: My feet are grounded on the river bed, while the current sloshes around my ankles, while the feelings (the water) hit me and then move past me but not affecting my steadiness. In this way I stay in the moment, remembering that emotions are just temporary, they can't hurt you, and don't get caught up in them. Staying in the moment means I'm not worried about what will happen afterwards, or getting stuck ruminating over a past I can't do anything about.

This, however, is hard when someone really pushes your buttons and gets on your nerves, which is bound to happen in any organisation. When we're under this kind of stress, many of us respond by ramping up our natural traits; the quiet person goes even quieter, the loud person gets even louder.[6] I also often see people react with anger or frustration as a default instead of how they really feel, which might be upset, disappointed or any other emotion tinted with 'sadness'.[7] We often tend to default to anger-based emotions because they're easier to access and make us feel less vulnerable. As a quiet leader, we need to resist these default responses and create mechanisms for ourselves to feel calm and tap into the real emotions we have, and then express them appropriately. Staying calm, though, is easier said than done. What really goes on inside when we're unable to do so, and how can we reduce the risk of getting carried away by someone else's emotional maelstrom?

# The science bit

I showed in Chapter 1 that extroverts are more responsive to external inputs and look outwards to others for attention and status,[8] which comes from having a more active dopamine reward system than introverts, and leads to a higher need for external validation and recognition from others.[9] Introverts, on the other hand, have stronger intrinsic motivation and are often self-starters.[10] This external focus means that extroverts are more excitable than introverts[11] and need to work harder to activate the parts of the brain that create calmness. As I mentioned in Chapter 11, the brain has different patterns that are incompatible; it's impossible to be angry and compassionate at the same time because these brain circuits run in two different patterns that can't be activated simultaneously. Similarly, the pattern for calmness can't be switched *on* if the circuit for anxiety isn't also switched *off* – the two are intrinsically linked. Therefore, reducing anxiety – which you can do by reducing cortisol (stress) – will make it easier to stay calm. This all takes place in our parasympathetic nervous system, where the vagus nerve carries information from our major organs such as our lungs to the brain. In essence, the brain interprets the signals from the body – it thinks 'my heart rate is high therefore I'm anxious'. We can therefore influence how calm we feel by manipulating our body to send signals of calmness to the brain (such as a slowing heart rate), as it's often easier to control our bodies than it is to control our brains (the information actually flows in both directions, and as long as we influence one of the two we can calm ourselves down). We can do this by doing breathwork that slows down the heart rate and tricks the brain into thinking we're relaxed, which then in turn helps us actually relax.[12] The exercise below is a good starting point. We can also do yoga, tai chi or qigong for the same effect, but deep breathing is much easier to do anytime, anywhere, and all have the same effect of triggering the calming reflex.

## Exercise

Take a deep breath through your nose, expanding your stomach as you do so, and without lifting your shoulders. This is the type of breathing that has the biggest impact as it avoids the shallow breaths that often ends with your shoulders around your ears (it's the chest expansion that makes you calmer). Hold the in-breath for 5 seconds, then exhale for 10. It should feel as if your belly has deflated fully. Repeat this multiple times. (It matters less how long you hold the in-breath, so long as the out-breath is longer – choose the duration that feels most natural, though I'd recommend at least 3 seconds on the in-breath to slow down your breathing sufficiently.)

# Create a calm environment

Interpersonal relationships can be difficult, especially when emotions are running high. It's not a case of just hoping for the best outcomes; the best interactions are the ones we bring conscious thought to; where we consider the impact of what's being said, and bring everyone on the same page without elevating anyone's blood pressure. This often becomes the role of the quiet leader. You can do this in different ways: Firstly, by how you respond personally through modelling the behaviours you'd like to see in others. People around you notice your reactions when you receive negative feedback, bad news, or an urgent and unexpected deadline. By being in control of your response, and handling the situation in a calm manner, not only do you model for those around you how they too should behave and they see it can be done, but if you manage to stay and – crucially – feel calm in a tense situation, others will also feel calm too. In tense situations, someone who's agitated often simply needs to vent, and for someone to listen to them doing so. The act of being listened to generally reduces the strength of their feeling and calms the situation down,[13] and it's virtually impossible for someone to maintain a high level of strong emotion over the course of an interaction if this isn't reciprocated and you stay calm.[14] I've outlined key ways of modelling calmness in the box below.

## How to model calmness

- Move less.
- Speak deliberately.
- Don't react, respond – use the pause.
- Don't raise your voice.
- Don't interrupt.
- Take deep breaths.
- Stay in the moment.
- Maintain curiosity.
- Don't make assumptions.

Secondly, you can create calm through the messages you explicitly send about the environment you expect to work in. As a quiet leader, the behaviour you encourage becomes your team culture, and when you create a culture of inclusivity and connectedness, colleagues also feel calmer. It's therefore important how you interact with your team as well as how they interact with each other. If you see something you'd like to adjust, you help them stay calm if you focus patiently on how you want to help them grow, what works already, and praise their effort if they work hard to improve – rather than expressing frustration and focus on the things that don't yet work so well.[15]

## Exercise

1. Think of something that makes you angry, and find a specific situation where you've encountered this feeling, for instance that person who overtook you while driving the other day.
2. Take a deep breath through your nose, expanding your stomach as you do so.

**3.** Think of a physical response that reflects calm; a facial expression, your posture, a gesture, or something else.

**4.** Reflect on how it feels to have this calming response.

**5.** Repeat this as close to a trigger scenario as possible, each time, until one day you're able to introduce the calm response while triggered.

# Hit the pause button

Although we want to remain calm in the face of stress, we don't want to be so calm and laid-back that we become passive. I'm talking about a purposeful calm, enough to create a pause and give you control over your own response. The famous quote from Viktor Frankl, the Holocaust survivor, comes to mind: 'Between stimulus and response there is a space'.[16]

$$\text{Situation} \quad + \quad \text{Pause} \quad = \quad \text{Response}$$
$$\text{(stimulus)} \qquad \text{(the space)}$$

It's this space we're trying to create so you can be intentional about your behaviour. This intention requires you to understand what you want to get out of a particular situation.[17] Imagine you're in a conversation with a team member about their performance in a client meeting where they weren't able to answer basic technical questions the client asked on a pitch, so you had to step in, and you want to avoid this happening again. Your objective is to help them improve, and therefore you give them some tips on how to handle it in future if they don't know the answer to a client's question, and give them advice about the types of questions likely to come up – you want to help them be as good as they can be. You'd also have the conversation while the pitch is still fresh in both your minds so they understand your comments clearly. If, on the other hand, you just want to let off some steam and make yourself feel better because you're frustrated the colleague hadn't prepared enough, you'd handle the conversation completely differently – you might make a comment about losing a client and decide not to share any advice (this option would almost certainly not lead to improved performance!).

---

## Questions to ask yourself during the pause

- What do I want to achieve?
- What do I need to communicate to achieve this goal?
- How best to communicate to achieve the goal?
- When would it be best to communicate, can it wait?

---

Use the space below to fill in your own scenario to see how your objective impacts your approach.

| Questions to ask yourself | Your response |
|---|---|
| What do I want from the interaction (e.g. improved performance, building relationship, find an answer, make a decision, persuade someone)? | |
| What are the points I need to communicate to achieve this? | |
| How do I best communicate (e.g. email, by phone, in person, body language, specific words to use)? | |
| When should I communicate (e.g. now, later, scheduled meeting, watercooler)? | |

In order to use the pause to full effect, you have to feel entitled to do so.[18] If you feel you have the right to take control of the conversation and insert a pause, it immediately helps you feel calmer, as shown in Figure 12.1. This feeling that you have the right to take control comes from a feeling of power – you're not dependent on anyone

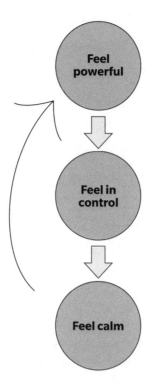

**Figure 12.1** Feeling powerful leads to calm and is self-perpetuating

else's behaviour or a particular response from them, you don't feel threatened or guilty; you feel grounded.

There's something very powerful about being able to slow down the pace of a conversation, and because it requires power to take up the space to do this, it requires some practice (especially if you don't belong to one of the majority groups in your organisation). It helps if you're comfortable with who you are, what you stand for and know your worth – all internally driven. You can also fool your body to feel more in control and more powerful by forcing a pause and taking a breath. A crucial element in this is to *respond* to your feelings and not *react* to them; I show the difference in the visual in Figure 12.2 – one is intentional and the other is automatic (responding uses the slow thinking brain systems we talked about in Chapter 2). If you feel small and powerless, it's easy to rush and panic, perpetuating the feeling of not being in control.[19] I've found it helps to have

| React | Respond |
|---|---|
| Instinctive and automatic | Deliberate |
| Affected by bias and history | Ability to override |
| Impulsive | Thoughtful |
| Emotional | Logical |
| Immediate | Delayed |
| Volatile | Stable |

**Figure 12.2** A response is different from a reaction

pre-prepared responses ready that give me the space I need to feel calm (it depends on the situation, but examples include 'that might be an idea', 'I agree with some of what you say', 'I don't see how that would work'). As long as you don't react immediately and breathe – you're giving your body and mind a chance to calm down.

# A permanent pause

It can be beneficial to make a pause permanent (many a time have I written a draft email only to never send it), but make sure you're doing it consciously and not to avoid a conflict that might be a necessary one to have. Being a quiet leader is about creating and using the pause, not about avoiding a response altogether when one is appropriate. To determine what requires a response and what you're better off letting pass by, the 'zoom in, zoom out' method developed by psychologist Richard Weissbound is a useful tool – it helps you calm down, consider the other person's view, and identify what's important.[20] Zooming in means first noticing what's going on inside yourself (e.g. 'I'm nervous about what my manager will think of me if I don't agree to her suggested deadline'), and next looking at the wider picture including the other person's perspective (zooming out). This helps you consider what else might be going on (maybe your manager is getting pressure from the board to deliver the report she's asking you about) and also to consider whether this will be important a year from now. This helps you better manage your time and improves relationships; not everything needs an immediate response, but you need to know what does. Not only will this help your calmness, but your team will also appreciate it if you're able to differentiate between what's a true emergency and what isn't – nobody likes to work the weekend only to be told on Monday that the input is no longer needed. It's a sign of a good quiet leader to be able to resist the temptation to take immediate action when one isn't necessary. This has benefits for quality as well: Rarely is the first solution that comes to mind the best one, and often those who panic are forced down a path of delivering quick fixes, which are usually no more than band aids over a problem that needs to be revisited again at some point in the future.[21] Taking no action is also an action, and knowing what type of action is needed, and when it isn't, will help you continue to stay calm. In the words of former US President and Founding Father Benjamin Franklin, who developed a list of thirteen virtues he recommended we all live by, one of which was tranquillity: 'Be not disturbed at trifles, or at accidents common or unavoidable'.[22]

---

## Exercise

Identify a situation where you feel under pressure to take immediate action. 'Zoom in' (focus and analyse) on your own perspective to understand this fully – what are the feelings underpinning your stress response? Is it anxiety, fear, guilt, something else? Then 'zoom out' to consider the wider perspective of those around you. Does this change your stress level?

# A section for self-reflection

------------------------------------------------

- In which situations do you find it hard to stay calm? Do these have anything in common?
- Which behaviours do you implicitly or explicitly approve of in your team?

------------------------------------------------

# Where do we go next?

---

If you only take one thing away after reading this book, I hope it's that you don't have to be loud to be a great leader. The loudest person isn't always the one who achieves the best results or has the greatest ideas. This is easily forgotten in a world where we too rarely listen to all the voices in the room and let ourselves be swayed by biases and outdated views of what good leadership looks like. These biases hold us back and lead to suboptimal performance in teams and organisations alike. While there's no single way of being a good leader, and more research is needed into the linkages between the brain and behavioural preferences, I've highlighted in this book a set of skills that are key to leadership in today's complex and interconnected world: Reflection and thoughtfulness; self-awareness; ability to actively listen and keenly observe; a willingness to learn and grow with the humility of knowing that no single person has all the answers; and a calmness and empathy that help steer choppy organisational and emotional waters. It's high time we recognise that there's no need to 'fix' the quiet among us; quiet leaders already have these skills we say we need and value. If we look out for the people who have these abilities already, and encourage everyone to leverage the quiet leader's skills, we'd eliminate the disconnect between what we say we want and what we promote in practice, avoiding the lazy view of 'good leadership' where we let ourselves be ruled by our reptilian brains that are fooled by dominating behaviours and other biases.

Throughout this, quiet leaders need to be recognised and promoted for the value they bring. This requires more of all of us, as it means we can no longer rely on our default, emotional reactions. This is ultimately for the best as the biases they are based on no longer serve us. Having a more conscious approach to what we consider good leadership, and recognising where these skills sit, will make us all better and elevate performance across the board. We'd be leveraging all skills available, not just those whose skills we can more easily see. This will ultimately lead to more inclusive corporate cultures where all groups can thrive, including those historically less visible and underrepresented.

The quiet, introverted person isn't automatically a better leader than the extrovert, but the quiet have skills that need to be recognised as strengths which everyone can learn from and replicate. In the process of doing so, we shift our view of what good looks like and level the playing field so we can all consciously choose the behaviour that best fits the situation at hand and which yields the best results for the outcome we want. Whether you label yourself an introvert or not, or something in between, our organisations will benefit if all skills – and those who showcase them – can flourish as we learn from each other. The list of skills a leader needs is much longer than any single book can cover in depth, and there are many other good resources on each individual skill; I recommend a read through the notes and references as a starting point to explore further.

As you complete the exercises in the book, and experiment with different behaviours in your day-to-day, don't expect perfection and a 100 per cent success rate. The work you're doing here can be hard; it's not easy to change the circuitry of the brain and adjust years, maybe decades, of behaviour and assumptions. So go easy on yourself, and keep trying. Your colleagues will thank you for it, and we will all perform better as a result.

# Notes
# and references

___

A large number of books and articles were consumed in the development and writing of this book, and I've been inspired by so many more over the years. I've attempted in the below to give as comprehensive a view as possible of those I've used as direct sources.

## What brought us here?

1  There are some exceptions to this, and I proudly stand on the shoulders of those who've championed the value of quiet before me, such as Dr Laurie Helgoe, Marti Olsen Laney, Susan Cain, Jennifer Kahnweiler and Megumi Miki (though, while recognising the value that quiet individuals bring, many of them also talk about what introverts need to do differently in order to fit in, which I don't subscribe to – it's the system that needs to be more inclusive).
2  I use the more common 'extro' spelling throughout, not the technical 'extraversion'.

# Chapter 1

1 Thom, Jamie (2020) *A Quiet Education*. Suffolk: John Catt Publishing, 25.
2 Quote by Malcolm Gladwell, flagged in Ibid.
3 The list of introverts in the public eye is based on several inputs, such as public statements by the individuals where they confirm that they consider themselves to be an introvert or they confirm traits associated with introversion; or they've been included on public lists of introverts inferred based on their behaviour or quotes from statements they've made publicly.
4 Helgoe, Laurie, PhD (2013) *Introvert Power* (2nd edition). Naperville: Sourcebooks, 7.
5 This is stated in almost all books on introversion used in this reading list.
6 For these definitions, I've primarily relied on: Laney, Marti Olsen, PhD (2002) *The Introvert Advantage*. New York: Workman Publishing; and Nettle, Daniel (2009) *Personality*. Oxford: Oxford University Press.
7 There are a large number of sources discussing the pros and cons of Myers Briggs. If you'd like to know more, an overview can be found in *Psychology Today* (https://www.psychologytoday.com/us/basics/myers-briggs).
8 Caroline Criado-Perez argues that a woman should be defined on her own terms and not simply as 'not a man'. This is similar to the extrovert default conceptually, but a major separate topic in its own right. You can read more in her 2019 book *Invisible Women* (London: Chatto & Windus), which I highly recommend.
9 Helgoe (2013), xxv.
10 Original work started by Creek, Jonathan and Arnold Buss in 1981 Shyness and Sociability in *Journal of Personality and Social Psychology* (1981), vol. 41, no. 2, 330–339, and subsequently updated and revised several times, most recently in 2020. Unrevised (pre-2020) version quoted in Granneman, Jenn (2017) *The Secret Lives of Introverts*. New York: Skyhorse Publishing, Inc., 38–44.

11 Helgoe (2013), 8.

12 Ibid., 6–7.

13 To aid my understanding of the science around what we know about brain activity associated with introversion and extroversion, I have relied on the following three books: *Personality* (pp. 93–103) by Daniel Nettle, *The Introvert Advantage* (pp. 65–92) by Martin Olsen Laney and *Introvert Power* (pp. 17–18) by Laurie Helgoe, PhD. If you're looking for something shorter, a good summary showing what we currently know about extroversion from brain imaging can be found in the paper *Personality Neuroscience: An Emerging Field With Bright Prospects* by DeYoung *et al.*, an international collaborative effort between researchers from Germany, Canada, USA, UK, Netherlands and Australia (representing universities such as UCL, University of Cambridge, McGill University and others), and also includes an interesting overview of the emerging field of personality neuroscience, which combines psychology and neuroscience. This paper was published in *Personality Science* 12 October 2022 and is available online from https://ps.psychopen.eu/index.php/ps/article/view/7269/7269.pdf), specifically p. 7.

14 Studies around introversion are referenced in Laney (2002) and Helgoe (2013). I have also used Davidson, Richard J. PhD and Sharon Begley (2013) *The Emotional Life of Your Brain.* New York: Hodder & Staughton; Agarwal, Pragya (2020) *Sway: Unravelling Unconscious Bias.* London: Bloomsbury; and others, to aid my understanding of the workings of the brain. I also used DeYoung *et al.* (2022) for the latest on brain imaging in relation to introversion and extroversion (see note 13 from this chapter for details).

15 Performed by Dr Debra Johnson and reported in the *American Journal of Psychiatry.* She's quoted in Laney (2002).

16 Nettle (2009, pp. 94–95) refers to several studies which show that extroverts are in a better mood after writing about positive experiences and seeing nice things on film, and fMRI scans show that extroverts have higher brain activity when seeing the positive images. The same results appear when they are anticipating

a positive reward. The same does not happen after negative experiences and images, therefore extroversion specifically relates to high sensitivity for positive reward. Both Laney and Nettle also refer to the genetic influence of having more than one copy of the long form of gene D4DR; however, I have omitted this as Nettle notes that studies to date haven't always been conclusive and replicable relating to this gene's impact on personality.

17 Note that Laney (2002) states that brain imaging shows that extroverts have a greater demand for dopamine and have a low sensitivity to it. However, Nettle (2009) states that brain imagining has shown that extroverts have high sensitivity to the positive emotions associated with dopamine, which appears to contradict Laney. By stating that extroverts have greater demand for and greater positive response to dopamine, I have attempted to reconcile these results, with heavier emphasis on Nettle's research, which is more recent and supported by DeYoung *et al.* I also want to flag that Nettle appears to assume, when he writes that extroverts have a greater responsiveness to the positive emotions associated with the 'buzz of company and excitement' (p. 93), that the extrovert's approach (company, activity, buzz) is the more positive, which seems another example of the extrovert bias. I think it's just as likely that introverts see different things as positive. All of this shows us that continued research is needed to understand the topic more fully.

18 Helgoe (2013), xxii; Laney (2002), 28.

19 Nettle (2009) does a great job of explaining in much more detail why these arguments are not valid, in particular see pp. 40–51.

20 **Being flattered and internalising negative messages:** Miki, Megumi (2020) *Quietly Powerful. M*ajor Street Publishing, 93, 95–96.

# Chapter 2

1 Helgoe (2013), 11; Miki (2020), 47.

2 **Seen as not active, doesn't matter if actions are right ones:** Miki (2020), 31. She's referring to Dr James Fox's book *How to*

*Lead a Quest.* The same point is also made in Dobelli, Rolf (2013) *The Art of Thinking Clearly.* London: Sceptre, 135.

3 I speak from personal experience – I've done a fair few of these throughout my corporate career.

4 There's recent research that recommends a move beyond the 'Big 5'; however, this work is still in its infancy. For more on the Big 5, see the American Psychology Association's summary (https://dictionary.apa.org/big-five-personality-model).

5 As of March 2024, the OED note that the word and its meaning is due an update; however, this has not yet taken place.

6 Halpern, David (2015) *Inside the Nudge Unit.* London: Penguin Random House. Based on Richard Thaler's research which showed that, for a number of reasons, humans tend to avoid making decisions away from the default.

7 Criado Perez (2019), 186–190.

8 The White House, https://www.whitehouse.gov/about-the-white-house/first-families/hillary-rodham-clinton/

9 **Not presidential enough:** Miki (2020), 108.

10 **First female nominee:** Center for American Women and Politics, 'Women Presidential and Vice-Presidential Candidates', https://cawp.rutgers.edu/facts/levels-office/federal-executive/women-presidential-and-vice-presidential-candidates-selected

11 There was likely also more than a small share of bias because she didn't follow the traditional housewife path for women in the 1970s, which would continue to haunt her during her own presidential campaign in 2008. This is a fascinating history in its own right. For more, see Carpentier, Megan, *The Guardian,* 18 October 2016 (https://www.theguardian.com/us-news/2016/oct/18/hillary-clinton-why-hate-unlikeable-us-election).

12 **Focus on negative with introversion and positive with extroversion:** Miki (2020), 60 and 93.

13 Helgoe (2013), 10–11.

14 **Black woman stereotype:** Motro, Daphna, *et al., Harvard Business Review Online,* 21 January 2022 (https://hbr.org/2022/01/the-angry-black-woman-stereotype-at-work).

15 **Internalising of negatives:** Miki (2020), 93–95.

16 For the content on heuristics in this book, I've primarily leveraged Agarwal (2020); Hans Roling (2018) *Factfulness*. London: Sceptre; and Daniel Kahneman (2011) *Thinking Fast and Slow*. London: Penguin Books.

17 Martin, Stephen and Joseph Marks (2019) *Messengers*. London: Penguin Random House, 100. They refer to work completed by Lukaszewski, Simmons, Anderson and Roney published in the *Journal of Personality and Social Psychology* in 2016.

18 Ibid., 121–142.

19 Agarwal (2020), 39.

20 Ibid., 11.

21 A rare example of where bias is positive is the bias we feel towards our children – that we see them as unique and amazing helps us raise and care for them. If you're interested in reading more, Pragya Agarwal takes us on a fascinating journey through the complexities of unconscious bias in her excellent book *Sway: Unravelling Unconscious Bias*. I can also recommend Daniel Kahneman's seminal read *Thinking Fast and Slow* for more on this.

22 As noted in Miki (2020), 106.

23 Ibid., 31.

24 Question raised by a young person sharing thoughts with Thom (2020), 28.

25 Summer, Melissa, *Myers Briggs Foundation, 2 January 2020* (https://www.themyersbriggs.com/en-US/Connect-With-Us/Blog/2020/January/World-Introvert-Day-2020).

26 Miki (2020), 153.

27 **Introverts making connections others haven't:** Miki (2020), 125.

28 **Introverts prepping and liaising ahead of meeting:** Ibid, 18.

29 **Experts also fooled:** Dobelli (2013), 95.

30 **Marking students:** Ibid., p. 96.

31 Ibid., p. 95. Wheel of fortune study was conducted by Amos Tversky.

32 Ibid., pp. 241–243.

33 He did this in 2018. Search anywhere on the internet for the vast amount of ridicule that followed, one of whom was Piers Morgan (subsequently racanted), *BBC, 16 October 2018* (https://www. bbc.co.uk/news/uk-45873664).

34 For confirmation bias, I've leveraged Dobelli (2013), 23–25; Agarwal (2020), 36, 152–180; Miki (2020), 71–72.

35 **Halo effect:** Dobelli (2013), 118–120 and 191.

36 Martin and Marks (2019), 87–88.

37 Laney (2002), 284–285.

38 **Confidence-appearing behaviours:** I've relied on Scouller, James (2016) *The Three Levels of Leadership.* Oxford: Management Books 2000 Ltd, 26; and Miki (2020), 102–105.

39 **Losing out on talent:** Miki (2020), 15.

40 **Dunning–Kruger effect:** Dobelli (2013), 222.

41 **We behave in ways that support our bias:** Miki (2020), 71.

# Chapter 3

1 **Not good at identifying good leadership:** Miki (2020), 102. She quotes Green, Taraki and Groenen (2006).

2 See in particular Laney (2002), Helgoe (2013) and Cain (2013).

3 To read more, I recommend starting with *Personality* by Daniel Nettle, *Introvert Power* by Laurie Helgoe, PhD and Marti Laney Olsen's *The Introvert Advantage*.

4 Using the studies above and the other resources referenced in this book, I have grouped together similar skills to a higher-level skills category. Introverts have a larger number of skills, such as planning ahead, detailed analysis and focus. However, I have focused on skills that can be logically considered to be necessary for leadership as opposed to being an individual contributor.

5 **Solitude is necessary:** This is documented by many, but I've relied mainly on Hammond, Claudia (2019) *The Art of Rest.* Edinburgh: Canongate, 176 and Miki (2020), 46.

6 Miki (2020), 133–137.

7 History.com editors, *History.com*, 'Neil Armstrong', 26 September 2023 (https://www.history.com/topics/space-exploration/neil-armstrong).

8 Scouller (2016) as well as my own corporate background.

9 Ibid., 33–34 and 38.

10 Scouller (2016) talks about servant leadership, referring to Robert Greenleaf's writings.

11 Miki (2020), 115–116.

12 *National Society for Leadership and Success,* 'Key Characteristics of Democratic Leadership' (https://www.nsls.org/blog/key-characteristics-of-democratic-leadership).

13 Bass, Bernard and Ronald Riggio (2005), *Transformational Leadership* (2nd edition). New York: Psychology Press (https://www.taylorfrancis.com/books/mono/10.4324/9781410617095/transformational-leadership-bernard-bass-ronald-riggio).

14 Scott, Kim (Unknown) *Our Approach* (https://www.radicalcandor.com/our-approach/).

15 Fayol, Henri (1949) *General and Industrial Management,* London: Pitman and Sons Ltd [Please note – this is the English translation, the book was originally published in French in 1916.].

  Drucker, Peter F. (1955) The *Practice of Management*, London: William Heineman Ltd

  Carnegie, Dale (1936) *How to win friends and influence people,* London: Vermillion

  Collins, James C. (2001) *Good to Great,* London: Random House

  Lencioni, Patrick (2002) *Five Dysfunctions of a team,* San Francisco: Jossey-Bass.

16 Miki (2020).

17 **Industrial Revolution:** Cable, Daniel M. (2019) *Alive at Work.* Boston: Harvard Business Review Press, 7.

18 **Extrovert bias is entrenched:** Cain, Susan (2013) *Quiet.* New York: Broadway Books, 1–7.

19 Marquet, L. David (2013) *Turn The Ship Around!* London: Penguin Random House, xxii.

20 Koh, Reena, *Business Insider,* 11 July 2023 (https://www.businessinsider.com/ai-generated-barbie-every-country-criticism-internet-midjourney-racism-2023-7).

21 Hern, Alex, *The Guardian,* 12 January 2018 (https://amp.theguardian.com/technology/2018/jan/12/google-racism-ban-gorilla-black-people)

22 Milmo, Dan and Alex Hern, *The Guardian*, 8 March 2024 'We definitely messed up: Why did Google AI tool make offensive historical images' (https://amp.theguardian.com/technology/2024/mar/08/we-definitely-messed-up-why-did-google-ai-tool-make-offensive-historical-images).

23 **40 per cent of US executives:** Grannemann, Jenn (2017) *The Secret Lives of Introverts.* New York: Skyhorse Publishing, Inc., 65.

# Chapter 4

1 I first came across the shoe analogy on LinkedIn. It was originally created by Jamie Shields, though I have made adjustments.

2 **Unique perspective improves performance:** Cable (2019), 57–58, 63–65, 76–77 and 79.

3 Some might find this illustration controversial (I did mention at the start that DEI language is tricky!). Some critics feel this image implies that the problem lies in the inherent biological characteristic of the short person who needs the box in the first place (height, of course, can be replaced with any biologically associated characteristic, like race, gender or introversion). I've chosen to nevertheless use this illustration because to me it shows visually in a way that would be harder to explain in words that the problem isn't anyone's biology; the real problem is the **fence** and the fence has been designed with one group in mind (the 'extrovert default' from Chapter 2). This visual reminds us that the fence is an artificial construct which we can also remove.

4 Helgoe (2013), 16.

5 Miki (2020), 120.

6 Gawande, Atul (2010) *The Checklist Manifesto*. London: Profile Books, 1–3.

7 **Darwin and Edison didn't work alone:** Dweck, Carol S. PhD (2006) *Mindset*. New York: Random House, 55–56.

8 Cable (2019), 76.

9 Cuddy, Amy (2019) *Presence*. London: Orion Books, 255 and 258.

10 Ibid., 255.

# Chapter 5

1 Potter, Ashley, *Warwick Business School, 17 November 2021* (https://www.wbs.ac.uk/news/putting-theory-into-practice-kuebler-ross-change-curve/).

2 Cable (2019), 134.

3 For more on the fascinating topic of neuroplasticity, see Richard J. Davidson and Sharon Begley's *The Emotional Life of Your Brain* and David Siegel's *Mindsight*. I have primarily used these two sources, as well as Gibson (2010), Nettle (2009) and Dweck (2006). I would also recommend Norman Doidge's *The Brain That Changes Itself*. There are also many great books about individual experiences of neuroplasticity; two of my favourites are *The Woman Who Changed Her Brain* (Barbara Arrowsmith-Young) and *The Man Who Mistook His Wife For a Hat* (Oliver Sacks).

4 Davidson and Begley (2013), 167.

5 Ibid.

6 Dweck (2006), 214.

7 Erikson, Thomas (2019) *Surrounded by Idiots*. New York: St. Martin's Publishing, 127.

8 Ibarra, Herminia (2015) *Act Like a Leader, Think Like a Leader*. Boston: Harvard Business Review Press.

9 Dweck (2006).

10 Syed, Matthew, *BBC*, 15 September 2015 (https://www.bbc.co.uk/news/magazine-34247629).

11 Cuddy (2016), 259.

12 Dweck (2006).

13  Johnson, Whitney (2018) *Build an A-Team*. Boston: Harvard Business Review Press, 110.

14  Erikson (2019), adaption sections throughout book.

15  **Take for granted skills that are easy:** Bregman, Peter (2018) *Leading with Emotional Courage*. Hoboken: Wiley, p. 150; Johnson (2018), 52 and 35.

16  Ibid., pp. 69–70.

17  Note that my focus is that we should leverage the best from each type of leader, and appreciating what the quiet leader brings, both on an individual level as well as in larger groups. This is not the same as situational leadership, but it does overlap in one sense: That we need to be conscious of which behaviours we choose to amplify and use.

18  Helgoe (2013), 227.

## Which areas should you focus on?

1  Using the studies above and the other resources referenced in this book, I have identified all leadership skills these authors and researchers define as specific to introverts, then grouped together similar ones and mapped each to a higher-level skills category. Introverts have a broader number of skills, such as planning ahead, detailed analysis, focus and being self-starters (internally motivated); however, I have limited my writing to skills logically considered to be necessary for leadership as opposed to those where introverts add value as individual contributors.

2  Johnson, Spencer (1998) *Who moved my cheese?* London: Vermilion.

## Chapter 6

1  Quote by the White Rabbit in Lewis Caroll's *Alice in Wonderland*, originally published in 1865.

2 This quote can't be proven as having come from Einstein, but I've kept it in as attributed to him due to how ingrained this is in popular psyche. For more about provenance, see *Quote Investigator,* 22 May 2014 (https://quoteinvestigator.com/2014/05/22/solve/?amp=1).

3 Cuddy, 2016, 250.

4 Honoré, Carl (2013) *The Slow Fix.* London: Collins, 56–70.

5 Marquet (2013), 91.

6 Ethical decision-making: Hammond (2019), 176.

7 Ellenberg, Jordan, *Medium.com*, 14 July 2016 (https://medium.com/@penguinpress/an-excerpt-from-how-not-to-be-wrong-by-jordan-ellenberg-664e708cfc3d This is an excerpt from *How Not To Be Wrong* (2015), New York: Penguin.

8 Atchley, Paul, *Harvard Business Review Online,* 21 December 2010 (https://hbr.org/2010/12/you-cant-multi-task-so-stop-tr).

9 Thom (2020), 38–88. He refers to research around 'cognitive load theory'.

10 **Reflection good for creativity:** Hammond (2019), 176.

11 Hammond (2019), 176.

12 Clifford, Catherine, *CNBC, 28 July 2019* (https://www.cnbc.com/amp/2019/07/26/bill-gates-took-solo-think-weeks-in-a-cabin-in-the-woods.html).

13 Miki (2020), 50 and 225; Hammond (2019), 184.

14 Hammond (2019), 169–170 and 174; Agarwal (2020), 53.

15 Hammond (2019), 169.

16 Ibid., 171–173.

17 Ibid., 171.

18 Ibid., 183–184.

19 Granneman (2017), 114–115.

20 You might be sceptical about me creating a link between high performance and meditation. If so, I recommend you read Steven Laureys MD *The No-Nonsense Meditation Book* (London: Bloomsbury), which outlines the scientific basis for meditation.

21 Thom (2020), 62. He refers to *The Organization Man* by William H Whyte (1956).

22 Miki (2020), 30–32; Honoré (2013).

23 **Word nuance is important:** Thom (2020), 77.

24 Hammond (2019), 183.

25 Miki (2020), 31.

# Chapter 7

1 Eurich, Dr Tascha (2017) *Insight: The Power of Self-Awareness in a Self-Deluded World.* London: MacMillan, 3. I highly recommend this book for a more in-depth look at the topic of self-awareness.

2 Scouller (2016), throughout, but especially 14, 246 and notes on p. 344.

3 Eurich (2017), 42–44.

4 Laney (2002), 197 and 204.

5 For a more detailed explanation, see Gartner (https://www. gartner.com/en/human-resources/glossary/johari-window).

6 Eurich (2017), 4–5 and 52.

7 Bunting, Michael (2016) *The Mindful Leader.* New York: Wiley, 28.

8 Scouller (2016), 277.

9 Ibid., throughout, but especially pp. 14 and 246 and notes on p. 344.

10 Eurich (2017), 52.

11 Scouller (2016), 304.

12 Eurich (2017), 58–59.

13 Ibid., 105–107.

14 Ibid., 68.

15 Scouller (2016), throughout but especially 14, 246 and notes p. 344.

16 Bregman (2018).

17 Sinclair, Dr Michael and Josie Seydel (2016) *Working With Mindfulness.* London: Pearson, 130–131.

18 Eurich (2017), 34.

19 Sinclair and Seydel (2016), 109–110.

20 Ibid., 110.

# Chapter 8

1 The other top response was Reflection, which came second. Total responses 73.
2 Scouller (2016), 50.
3 Poumpouras, Evy (2020) *Becoming Bulletproof.* New York: Simon & Schuster, 149–167.
4 Sinclair and Seydel (2016), 122.
5 Kahnweiler, Jennifer B. (2018) *The Introverted Leader* (2nd edition). Berrett-Koehler Publishers, Inc.; Miki (2020).
6 Kahnweiler (2018).
7 Helgoe (2013).
8 Ekman, Paul (2003) *Emotions Revealed.* London: Orion Books, 15.
9 Bunting (2016), 7.
10 This is a famous mindfulness exercise which can be found in a lot of training materials and courses, usually using asking you to eat a raisin and continuing to notice texture, taste etc.
11 Bunting (2016), 11.
12 Poumpouras (2020), pp. 149–167.
13 Ibid., pp. 144–145.
14 This experiment is described in Dobelli (2013), 15; Agarwal (2020), 34.
15 Poumpouras (2020), 182–185.
16 Helgoe (2013), 140.
17 Eurich (2017), 40–41.
18 Kahneman (2011), 23–24.
19 Grannemann, Jenn (2017) *The Secret Lives of Introverts.* Skyhorse Publishing, Inc., 276

# Chapter 9

1 Granneman (2017), 94.
2 Helgoe (2013), 227.
3 Kahnweiler (2018), 10.
4 Miki (2020), 60.

5 Blanchard, Kenneth, et. al. (1989) *The One Minute Manager Meets the Monkey.* New York: Morrow and Company, Inc., 77 and Jennifer B. Kahnweiler (2013), *Quiet Influence.* San Francisco: Berrett-Koehler Publishers, Inc.

6 Erikson (2019), 61.

7 Cuddy (2016), 81.

8 Bregman (2018), 65.

9 In this way, we proved the research studies right: We weren't being creative and all our answers were cumulative from the original wrong one. The right theme was 'stone' which – when added to the end of each original answer – created a new meaning (Yellow-stone, Sharon Stone etc).

10 Miki (2020), 121.

11 Helgoe (2013), 146.

12 Bregman (2018), 63–70.

13 Cable (2019), 131 and 133.

14 Cuddy (2016), 81–82.

15 Granneman (2017), 163.

16 Cuddy (2016), 81.

17 I first learned of this exercise while on a silent meditation retreat at The Barn Retreat Centre (run by The Sharpham Trust) in Totnes, Devon, in 2012. It's a wonderful place and I highly recommend a visit to any of their retreats – they run many different ones throughout the year, and not all are silent ones.

18 Cuddy (2016), 79.

19 Bregman (2018), 65.

20 Erikson (2019), 1.

21 Kahnweiler (2013), 78–84.

22 **First step of interaction:** Pollard, Matthew with Derek Lewis (2018) *The Introvert's Edge.* American Management Association, 72–75.

# Chapter 10

1 **Components of humility:** Dweck (2006), 20–21, 110; Cable (2019), 125; Miki (2020), 109–110.

2 Kahnweiler (2018), 3; Miki (2020), 20.

3 Cain (2013), 54–55.

4 Kahnweiler, Jennifer B., PhD (2016) *The Genius of Opposites*. Berrett-Koehler Publishers, Inc., 39.

5 Groskop, Viv (2018) *How to Own the Room*. London: Bantam Press, 32–33, 36.

6 **Inner confidence to meet goals:** Bregman (2018), 10.

7 Groskop (2018), 29–30.

8 Laney (2002), 197.

9 Pink, Daniel (2013) *To Sell Is Human*. London: Canongate, 71–73.

10 **Types of humility:** Marks and Martin (2019), 167–168.

11 Granneman (2017), 237.

12 Scouller (2016), 34–35.

13 Grant, Adam, Francesca Gino and David A. Hofmann, *Harvard Business Review Online*, 10 December 2010 (https://hbr.org/2010/12/the-hidden-advantages-of-quiet-bosses). Extroverts are better at leading passive employees. We don't yet fully understand the cause and effect of this dynamic, that is whether employees become more proactive when they have an introvert as a leader, or if the introverted leader hires proactive employees to a larger degree.

14 Laney (2002), 204. The famous *The Wisdom of Crowds* by Surowiecki, James (2016) is also relevant here and his studies show that introverts are right to take inputs not just from ourselves.

15 **Circle of competence:** Dobelli (2013), 52–53.

16 Granneman (2017), 237.

17 Kahnweiler (2013), 85–87.

18 Marquet, (2013), 23–25 talks about his role in asking questions of the team. The list in this book evolved out of Marquet's.

19 Cable (2019), 125.

20 Details of the study are included in Eurich (2017), 164–166.

21 Bregman (2018), 13.

22 Ibid., p. 14.

# Chapter 11

1 Scouller (2016), 205.

2 Kahnweiler (2013), 76.

3 Poumpouras (2020), 150.

4 Siegel, Daniel (2011) *Mindsight*. London: One World, 62; and Eurich (2017), 40.

5 Ekman (2003), 180. Pink (2012) outlines the difference between empathy and perspective-taking (p. 73); as does Eurich (2017), 40.

6 Slingerland, Edward (2014) *Trying Not To Try*. Edinburgh: Canongate, 117.

7 Martin and Marks (2019), 87.

8 Ekman (2003), 180.

9 Slingerland (2014), 115–118.

10 Nettle (2009), 155–156.

11 Ibid., 157.

12 Slingerland (2014), 117.

13 Siegel (2011), 62.

14 Davidson and Begley (2012), 80 and 127.

15 This is covered in many of the books on this reading list; however, for my understanding of this topic I've relied mainly on Agarwal (2020), 69–101; Slingerland (2014), 209–210; Davidson and Begley (2012), 214 and 219–220.

16 Davidson and Begley (2012), 184–224, especially 214.

17 I also learned of this one from The Sharpham Trust back in 2012.

18 Gilbert, Paul (2010) *The Compassionate Mind*. London: Constable, 87.

19 Davidson and Begley (2013), 244–245.

20 **In-group bias and oxytocin spray test:** Huffington, Arianna (2014) *Thrive*. New York: Harmony Books, 237–238. Other sources in this list also mention this experiment.

21 Agarwal (2020), 75. I have somewhat simplified this research for our needs, as there are situations where in-group bias can be overridden.

22 Martin and Marks (2019), 203–204.

23 Quoted in Thom (2020), p. 206, and taken from a speech given by Barack Obama in 2011 (https://obamawhitehouse.archives.gov/the-press-office/2011/01/12/remarks-president-barack-obama-memorial-service-victims-shooting-tucson).

24 Martin and Marks (2019), 203.

25 Poumpouras (2020), 239; Scouller (2016), 50.

26 I have primarily leveraged Bregman (2018), Scouller (2016), and Emma Seppälä and Kim Cameron *Harvard Business Review Online*, 1 December 2015 (https://hbr.org/2015/12/proof-that-positive-work-cultures-are-more-productive). This is also alluded to in Cuddy (2016), Bunting (2018) and Gilbert (2010).

27 Thom (2020), 111.

28 Gilbert (2010), 94–95.

29 Huffington (2014), 67.

30 Eurich (2017), 52.

31 Martin and Marks (2019), 202–203.

32 Ibid., 199–200.

33 Pink (2013), 69.

34 Davidson and Begley (2012), 55; Martin and Marks (2019), 200.

35 Siegel (2011), 63.

36 Ibid., 62.

37 Empathy maps are traditionally used in computer sciences to access the perspective of the end user, a wonderful example of overlap across two traditionally separate disciplines, coding and psychology.

## Chapter 12

1 Kahnweiler (2018), 126–127.

2 Dobelli (2013), 177.

3 Helgoe (2013), 13.

4 Kahnweiler (2018), 126–127.

5 Thom (2020), 112.

6 Kahnweiler (2016), 63.

7 I recommend looking up 'emotion wheel' to understand the base emotions and to expand your vocabulary around feelings – it's a very interesting, albeit separate, topic.

8 Granneman (2017), 24.

9 Laney (2002), 71–73.

10 Ibid., 191.

11 Kahnweiler (2018).

12 Cuddy (2016). 189–190.

13 Bregman (2018), 65.

14 Thom (2020), 112.

15 Kahnweiler (2018), 126–127; Dweck (2006), 108–143.

16 Viktor Frankl (1959) *Man's Search for Meaning.* London: Random House. Quoted in Eurich (2017).

17 Bregman (2018), 98–99 and 162–163.

18 Cuddy (2016), 156. The visual is adapted from the narrative in her book.

19 Ibid.

20 This method is described in Eurich (2017), p. 41.

21 Honoré (2013), 91 and 108.

22 **Franklin quote**: Eurich (2017), 25.

# Index